First published in December 2014

Bill Mattos has asserted his moral right
to be identified as the author of this work.

A catalogue record for this book is
available from the British Library

ISBN 978 0 85733 481 7

Library of Congress control no. 2014930863

Published by Haynes Publishing,
Sparkford, Yeovil, Somerset BA22 7JJ, UK
Tel: 01963 442030 Fax: 01963 440001
Int. tel: +44 1963 442030 Int. fax: +44 1963 440001
E-mail: sales@haynes.co.uk
Website: www.haynes.co.uk

Haynes North America Inc.
861 Lawrence Drive, Newbury Park,
California 91320, USA

While every effort is taken to ensure the accuracy
of the information given in this book, no liability can
be accepted by the author or publishers for any loss,
damage or injury caused by errors in, or omissions
from the information given.

Printed in the USA by Odcombe Press LP,
1299 Bridgestone Parkway, La Vergne, TN 37086

THE ESSENTIAL GUIDE TO
ALL KINDS OF SKIING

BILL MATTOS

GETTING STARTED ▪ EQUIPMENT ▪ TECHNIQUES ▪ SAFETY ▪ COMPETITION

CONTENTS

INTRODUCTION

Hi, my name's Bill Mattos. Nice to meet you. I want to share with you what I've learned, not just about 'how to do' skiing, but about the whole process of going skiing.

It's often said that you can't learn to ski from a book. Most existing books on skiing do start by mentioning this, in fact, so it's a source of some confusion to me that they usually proceed almost immediately to try to teach you just that.

What you can learn from a book is to understand skiing. What is it, where does it come from, how does it work? What are the different types of skiing and how can I go about experiencing them and learning how to be awesome? Or just safe and basically OK at them. That's enough for most people.

Different types of skiing? Yes, there are many, a point that most of the books I've come across entirely omit to mention, filling their pages instead with insane amounts of technical detail about the one type of skiing (that admittedly most people do) that their authors are expert in and which, commercially speaking, people who want to have a go at sliding downhill are funnelled into without having the chance to question it at all.

In fact, when I read most books on skiing, what strikes me most is all the stuff they leave out. Which is a shame, because that is the kind of info that people really want and need! Where to go skiing, how to use ski lifts, tips to avoid injury and to feel safe around other skiers. Which part of the mountain to ski on at certain times of day. That kind of thing. So I've made sure to include all that here.

I don't claim to be a top expert at any sort of skiing. I'm just a person who lives in the mountains and, since I'm surrounded by the white stuff for nearly half the year, I've acquired a handful of skills (and a cupboard full of gear) to make the best use of whatever the day throws at me. I'm also lucky enough to be surrounded by lots of other mountain people, many of whom are excellent instructors, competitors or simply masterful protagonists of the art of using gravity to look cool and have a wicked time in the snow. So what follows is the sum of their wisdom. And some of our mistakes...

Bill Mattos
December 2014

I've designed this book to be first and foremost an interesting and entertaining read. Most of the sections will stand up on their own, meaning that if you need to know something that has gone before, or is to follow, there will probably be a cross-reference along the lines of '(see p237)'. There isn't a page two hundred and thirty-seven; that was just an example.

What this means is that if you flick through the book and something takes your fancy, you should be able to make sense of it pretty easily. Any words you come across that are new or alien to you should be included and explained in the glossary at the end (page 184). See what I did there? However, I've also had this brilliant idea that's handy if you're pushed for time. Reading this on the plane on your way to the snow, for instance! And it's called:

> **NEVER FORGET THAT THE BEST SKIER IS ALWAYS THE ONE WHO'S HAVING THE MOST FUN (SAFELY)!**

DON'T BE TOO SERIOUS!

Don't get me wrong. Skiing is awesome. People (a lot of people) get hooked on skiing, and live their whole year behind a desk looking forward to the week they can hit the hill. But the same thing that makes it so addictive also has a dark side. Some people take skiing pretty seriously. Too seriously, sometimes. Just as I once saw two men almost come to blows because one said something derogatory about Pamela Anderson's character in *Baywatch*, and by a similar virtue many people will become quite incensed if you say something bad about their favourite football team, I once ended up in a very awkward situation in a bar for saying that some technical detail of skiing technique 'didn't really matter...'.

One of the challenges of this book is to explain techniques without bias towards what type of skis you might be using. You may be on cross-country skis or super fat carvers. The techniques that were developed on fairly straight 'oldschool' skis have to some extent been superseded by modern hyper-parabolic sidecut. But on the other hand, someone may invent something new the moment this book goes to print. So, I have taken a holistic approach where possible and qualified certain statements where I must.

TERMINOLOGY

I have been for many years a writer, and even longer than that involved in outdoor sports, but I can honestly say I have never come across a sport where there is so much variation in the terms and expressions that are used for things, and so many different opinions about the correct way to do it. I'm not surprised that the 'stem christie' has fallen into disuse, because there seems to be no real consensus about what one actually is!

Skiing is an ever-developing sport, and rapid changes in equipment lead to constantly evolving technique. It is also a very ancient sport, so there are some traditions and protocols that temper this evolution with the old guard's 'right way to do it'. Never forget that the best skier is always the one who's having the most fun (safely)!

HOW NOT TO BE A TOTAL NUMPTY – TOP TEN (OR SO) TIPS!

In no particular order:

1 Do up your pocket zips (and/ or ventilation zips) if it's snowing, or you're powder/off-piste skiing, or you are likely to fall down for any reason.

2 Do not wear your goggles on top of your head (they steam up).

3 Do not ski in sunglasses except on safe cross-country trails. You may be awesome and never fall, but that's no consolation when a maniac or a beginner skis into you and you lose an eye.

4 Do not drop your stuff while riding on a chair lift. This includes hats, goggles, gloves, ski poles (and best of all cellphones which have a special way of vanishing into the snow).

5 Do not be the cause of an accident. At low speed it's hard to hurt anyone, but if you want to go fast, go away from other people, and no matter how skilful you are, don't swoosh into the lift line/queue like a victorious downhill champion. It's just rude!

6 Do learn the rules of the road – see page 94.

7 Be mindful of the conditions, and your own state of mind. One thing I've noticed about all adventure sports is that as conditions vary, so do our needs. You have to make sure that your ability and your equipment is appropriate on the day. It's quite easy to get fired up about what you want to do, and allow that to displace in your mind the fact that you are too tired, not correctly dressed, or just plain not good enough to pull it off!

8 Do not stand about in the middle of the piste, or below the brow of a hill where you can't be seen.

9 Don't ski stuff that's too difficult for your ability or try to convince others to do so. 'I made it down this double-hard, mogul-infested black run' is not a status thing if you did it on your arse, or looking like Bambi on ice.

10 Language. It's natural to be excited when you're in a wonderful place with your friends or family and doing something as awesome as skiing. A little whooping and cheering is not inappropriate, in fact it could be described as *de rigueur*! It is not nice, however, to take the sort of colourful language or ribaldry that might arise in the bar onto the slopes with you. Skiing is a family sport, with impressionable children aged three and upwards to be found even on that steep bit that you and your mates think is hardcore. Don't let them grow up thinking everyone from your part of the world is a moron!

TYPES OF SKIING AND SKIERS

Pull a skiing book at random off the shelves these days, and I suspect it may well be about one sort of skiing in particular. Admittedly, the type of skiing that most people end up getting involved in if they don't actually live in the snow... I can't deny that. But it seems to me to send an odd message. That type of skiing is often called 'downhill' skiing, an odd nomenclature to my mind, because most forms of skiing include quite a bit of going downhill. It's just that this type of skiing never really takes place uphill. Perhaps the reason. I may end up using the expression myself, but generally if I refer to downhill skiing, it means I am talking about skiing downhill, whatever type of skis or techniques are involved. Another term that is often used for it is 'Alpine' skiing. What it's almost never called is 'fixed heel' skiing, which

is odd, because all the other methods on this page involve freeing the heel some time/way or other!

'NORMAL SKIING' (ALPINE SKIING)

This includes snowblades, traditional straight skis, fat carvers, super fat powder skis, and twin tip freeskis, but the thing they all have in common is that they are downhill-only disciplines, using heavy, stiff boots with the soles locked down onto the skis to deliver maximum power and control. Because of this, ski lifts have to be used to go back up the hill. Ski lifts are not free, so it's clear that this type of skiing is where the money is to be made!

TELEMARK SKIING

Named after the town in Norway where it originated, telemark (see page 130) is for many practitioners the original discipline of skiing with a capital S. Sliding with the heel released for more functional rotation and to slow the descent, telemarking was developed by a carpenter in the 19th century. As better ski and boot technology facilitated turning with a fixed heel, telemarking was overtaken by alpine-style skiing, but it is enjoying a resurgence now, as many skiers seek a more aesthetic yet physically demanding discipline.

CROSS-COUNTRY SKIING (XC)

Cross-country skiing (see page 126) uses skinny, lightweight skis and boots that are closer to ordinary high-top trainers than anything, and is usually practised in specially made tracks and trails. The expert cross-country skier is usually equal to any terrain, however.

TOURING/RANDO/ADVENTURE SKIING

This species uses skis that are basically alpine skis, but usually very lightweight and suited to the backcountry, combined with special bindings that release at the heel to allow a cross-country walking action. Combined with 'skins' this allows the tourer to go uphill and, as the saying goes, 'earn the turns', locking the boots down for an alpine-style descent.

At the extreme, adventure skiers add spiked crampons to their bindings to ascend even more extreme terrain.

SIT SKI (HANDISKI)

Many people with reduced mobility enjoy skiing in a sitting position using a sit ski. Known in Europe as handiski, this style usually employs small ski-like attachments on the poles instead of the usual 'baskets', and a spring suspension system connecting one or two skis to the seat. The rider is strapped to the seat with a lap belt, and can deliver excellent power transmission for high performance carving!

Carving, racing and even jumping and freestyle are possible for the expert handiskier! Those who don't have the mobility to control a sit ski on their own can still enjoy the thrill of downhill skiing!

Skiing, even as we know it today, is a little more ancient than it appears. Cave drawings estimated at 5000BC that depict skiers using a single pole were found in Rødøy in Norway, and a wooden ski of at least that age was discovered in a bog 1,200km north-east of Moscow. There's pictorial evidence of skis in 2,000-year-old Roman mosaics, and since that time skis have cropped up all over the Northern hemisphere.

The word 'ski' as we use it today comes from a Norse word meaning wooden stick, and in Norwegian it continues to be used in words referring to split wooden items. So nowadays, when English speakers use words like 'planks' or 'sticks' to refer to skis, it is not as modern and colloquial a slang as it seems!

It's pretty clear that skiing developed from the discovery that tying sticks or branches to one's feet made it easier to walk around in the snow. From this we get the principle of the snowshoe but also that if one accidentally made a snow plank that slid along the snow easily instead of gripping the way a piece of brush would then it might not be such a good snowshoe but it would be less effort to move along, especially downhill.

From there, it's not a big leap to fashion something that resembles a modern ski, and we already have the evidence that our Mesolithic (Middle Stone Age) ancestors had done this. How they were attached to the feet will no doubt have varied, and sadly the oldest ropes and bindings, being made of reeds or twisted bark, have not survived, but the oldest of those that do imply that skiers experimented with tying the front of the foot to the ski with one or more cords.

ASYMMETRIC SKIING

Right up until the beginning of the 20th century, Finnish and Swedish skiers often used one long ski for gliding with a shorter one for kick propulsion. If they'd figured this out, it seems odd to me that they felt that two shorter skis would not be 'skateable' at the time. But maybe at least one long ski was necessary for the terrain, and two would have been hard to skate.

SINGLE SKIING

The mono ski might have looked like a newfangled invention in the 1970s, and a precursor to snowboarding perhaps, but in fact prehistoric seal hunters in Arctic regions used a single long ski (3–4 metres long) to traverse the ice and to bridge cracks and crevasses. With only one ski, it made sense to propel oneself with a paddle or spear.

Early skiers used one pole, which of course probably doubled as a spear or a staff. The first known depiction of a two-pole skier was from 1741, in Lapland. in a 1748 book by Hergstrom.

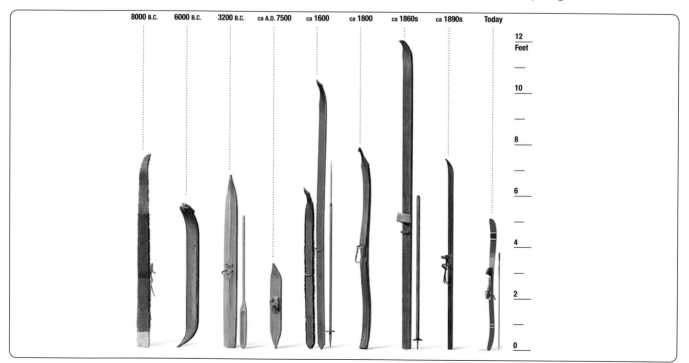

↑ The statue of Sondre Norheim overlooking his beloved snowfields of Telemark in Norway.

It's a little unclear whether 'Telemark'-style skiing was a precursor to fixed-heel skis, or whether they developed separately and were preferred in different places according to different needs or snow

conditions. Certainly a glance at any historic wooden skis implies that it was difficult to tie down the feet, so a certain amount of heel lift was inevitable. What we do know is that in the 1840s a Norwegian called Sondre Norheim from the Telemark region developed a binding with a strong heel loop, which allowed the heel to lift in the accustomed way but delivered much better response and power transmission to the ski. His aggressive style of skiing, characterised by hard turns and jumping, rapidly spread through the Telemark region and beyond. That's why we call this style 'telemarking', and that's why Sondre Norheim is often described as the father of modern skiing.

Norheim's aggressive style also gives us skis with rather more technical design features. The artisans of Telemark began to make skis with camber, more flex and a noticeable sidecut, enabling them to turn using leg and foot steering and body language. Prior to this, much of the steering effort had come from dragging a pole in the snow.

The first metal skis (solid aluminium) were introduced in the 1930s but the earliest use of separate metal edges with wooden or composite skis appears to be even later. Having said that, the use of bone for edges was probably tried off and on for a century before that. Now that we ski on metal rails, however, it's hard to see how anyone managed without them. A quick jaunt on modern plastic cross-country skis with no proper edges is enough for most people.

Skipping forward quickly now, the biggest changes in skiing in the 20th century were the widespread use of lifts, making downhill alpine skiing on steep terrain the most accessible form of the sport, and the rapid evolution of skis and boots.

Influenced by the development of snowboards, in the late 20th century skis became wider and wider, with ever more extreme sidecut, until most alpine skiers were using some variant of the fat hyper-parabolic carvers we see today.

→ ↓ A pair of wooden skis from the 1920s – they have an interesting prow-shaped design at the tip, and a groove underneath like a modern cross-country ski.

↑ An all-mountain ski from the 1990s – long and with moderate sidecut.

↑ The equivalent ski in the early 21st century was shorter and more rounded, with a dramatic hyperbolic sidecut.

TELEMARK

In 19th century Christiania (the old name for Oslo), the arrival of skiers from Telemark, with their better equipment and technique, blew a fresh wave of ideas through the skiing population. The traditional skiers had an ungainly style, and 'rode the stick', using it as a lever, or a brake, and for support. They fell often, whereas there was great shame associated with falling in Telemark. The Telemarkers had an elegant stance and skied faster. They also jumped higher and longer, and were able to do so without much use of the stick. Critically, they also glided effortlessly on the flat and uphill, instead of 'marching' on their skis by lifting them out of the snow. Skiing was changed forever.

CHAPTER ONE

FOR STARTERS

HOW SKIS WORK

Before we go too much further, I think it would be a good idea to look at how skis actually function, because it's more than a little counter-intuitive and even people who can already ski often have no idea about it. What makes a ski slide downhill, and what makes it respond to the skier's body language in order to steer, and stop? Read on...

Snow and ice is not inherently slippery. It's quite sticky, actually, as you can sometimes see when snow lands on your clothing, and the fact that anything you put down on the snow tends to sink into it only adds to the snow's disinclination to encourage motion. Alternatively, pick up an ice-cube straight from the ice-maker. See how it sticks to your fingers? That's the same effect – snow, you see, is made up of snowflakes which in turn are made of ice crystals. The reason skis slide downhill so readily is twofold. Firstly, the 'soles' of the skis have quite a large surface area, so that stops them from sinking into the snow as much as your feet would normally do.

Second, as the sole or 'base' of the ski presses onto the tips of the ice crystals beneath, it melts them, forming droplets of water which act as roller bearings, making it temporarily very slippery. As they come off the back of the ski they freeze again pretty much instantly. That's why snow that people have skied on is very different from fresh. We'll go into the complicated physics stuff later on, but for now we're ready to slide and that's all that matters.

As well as a base that's designed to do this slippery melting thing really well, skis also have 'edges'. These are designed to bite into the snow and mostly stop the ski from going sideways. That's why you can't turn them just by trying to twist your feet. We'll find out more about that later, too.

GRAVITY

I said we wouldn't do the physics lesson here, but there's one basic thing to understand about gravity (if you're geeky enough to know all about vectors, you can skip this bit). We kind of have the power to redirect gravity using obstructions. OK, that isn't strictly scientific, so let me say this: if we jump off a cliff we fall 100% straight down. If we are on more of a slopey mountain, we can't fall straight down

Skis sink/bite into the snow and hence redirect gravity/ momentum in the direction they are pointing.

GRAVITY

because the ground is in the way, but a smaller percentage of the gravity is still able to push us down the slope. The less steep the slope becomes, the smaller the percentage of gravity is pushing us downhill and the greater the part of it is just pressing us against the ground causing friction, so we 'fall' slower.

In the same way as the ground can redirect our motion, so can the sides of the skis. Because of their sharp edges, they won't go sideways without a good deal of trickery, so whatever forces are acting upon them are 'redirected' in the direction that the skis are pointing.

That, my friends, is how skis work.

FALL LINE

DIRECTION OF TRAVEL

➔ Gravity acts downwards. The natural direction of travel is down the hill. The edged skis bite into the hill and redirect this direction of travel. Simple.

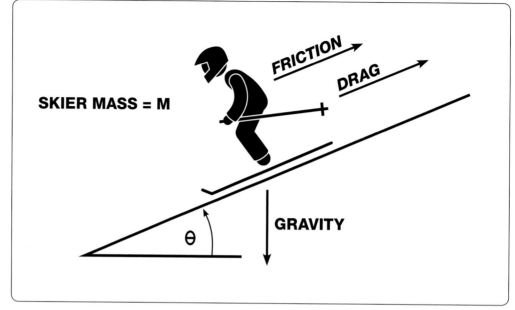

SKIER MASS = M

FRICTION

DRAG

GRAVITY

θ

So, the skis slide on the surface of the snow because the pressure and friction of the base against the snowflakes raises the temperature at the contact points and fuses and melts snow crystals. This means that you're sliding on a microscopic film of liquid. This happens in a microsecond, and immediately after the passage of the skis the particles of water freeze again as they return to their original temperature.

You may notice that the snow in the grooves left by the skis is shiny and polished by this process and can sometimes be almost mirror-reflective in the sun. This is because the microscopic tips of the snow 'flakes' have melted and filled in much of the space in between.

The odd thing about this whole situation is that the melting is caused mostly by friction, and it is this very friction that melts the snow and makes the resulting combination almost frictionless! In this sense, skis (or snowboards or sledges) are rather exceptional. Experience over thousands of years helped snow travellers of all persuasions to work out what slides the best, and it turns out that polishing the skis is not the answer. Modern tests have been performed using bases coated with Teflon™, the most frictionless solid known to man, and they are slower than traditional skis. Why? Because there is not enough friction to melt the snow to provide a slippery surface. Weird, huh? In fact, modern skiers apply a sticky kind of wax to the bottom of the skis to produce the perfect friction level for ski performance.

The base of your skis is made from a fairly common plastic material called polyethylene using a technique called sintering (sinterizing in the US). This is a method for making shapes out of powder by atomic diffusion. In most sintering processes, the powdered material is held in a mould and then heated to a temperature below the melting point. The atoms in the powder particles diffuse across the boundaries of the particles, fusing the particles together and creating one solid piece. Because the sintering temperature does not have to reach the melting point of the material, it retains a quality and purity that is higher than that of traditional moulding, but there is another reason too. Plastic materials are formed by sintering for applications that require materials of specific porosity. Sintered plastic is used for ski bases because it has ultra-high molecular weight while remaining porous, and can be ground to a surface finish that is fairly smooth, but not shiny or slippery by any means. The porous texture allows wax to be retained within the structure of the base material, thus providing a durable wax coating.

WAX, YOU SAY?

The special sticky wax molecules have been found to be perfect to melt just the right amount of snow for skiing, and to cause the water thus formed to bead into droplets of the right size to work well as 'bearing'. When the wax finally wears out, the skier can sense that the skis slow down dramatically. Different waxes are available for different snow temperatures, such is the complexity of the way the whole thing works. It's possible that someone could invent a ski base material that didn't need waxing, but then you'd need different skis for different snow conditions. With wax, this isn't necessary. More about waxing in a later chapter (see page 47).

Cross-country skis have a special property. We want them to slide forwards as well as downhill skis but to stick when you push them backwards. This helps to go uphill or to keep them moving forwards on the flat. This can be achieved by a special waxing strategy that is covered later too, or by 'scales' printed on part of the base. The latter type of skis are called 'waxless' or 'wax free' but that's a bit of a misnomer. You still have to wax part of the ski to make them fast, but it's less work than the special treatment that traditional XC skis require.

The centre part of the ski has a magic grip area made with a special finish or pattern, or else it is waxed with a special grip wax.

Skis vary enormously depending on what type of skiing they are designed for. It's a far cry from the early pioneers of recreational and competitive skiing, who used one pair of skis for everything, and wore the same boots that they used for walking, and probably for church on Sundays!

There are, however, a number of features that are common to nearly all skis, and this diagram should help you to familiarise yourself with them. The photo shows an alpine ski because that is by far the most common kind, but most other skis vary only in their dimensions, materials and the way in which the binding functions.

1. **Tip**
2. **Tail**
3. **Tip/tail protection.** These are common on hire skis but still found on other types. They make the skis safer in an accident and, most importantly, in the lift queue!
4. **Edge**
5. **Sidecut**
6. **Binding**
7. **Sole or base**
8. **Anti-friction device (AFD)**
9. **Binding release force setting** (DIN gauge) (Hergstrom, P (1748)(Hergstrom, P (1748)
10. **Upturn**

⬆ **Telemark binding complete with leash.**

⬆ **XC binding.**

⬆ **A twin-tip ski has an upturn at the tail that is much the same as that at the tip.**

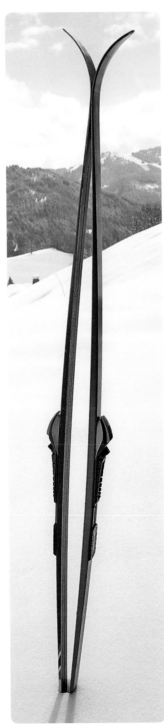

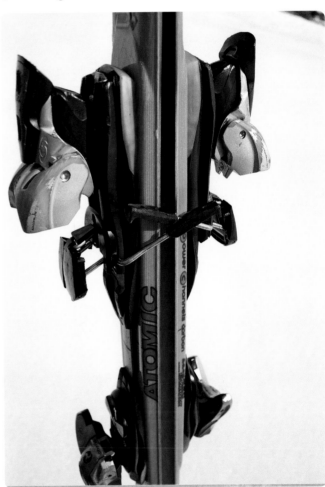

⬆ **Brake levers can also be used to lock the skis together for carrying.**

⬅ **Camber.**

SKI LENGTH

All-mountain skis are typically sized so that standing on end they come somewhere between your chin and the top of your head. But it's possible to ski on anything between snowblades that are waist high through downhill racing skis that are well over head height. So let's not get too hung up on it.

Even cross-country ski length varies a lot, from less than your height to way over, so be sure to consult the manufacturer's guidelines for your weight.

⬆ **Sometimes, ski dimensions are specified like this – the widest part of the tip, the narrowest bit of the waist, and the widest part of the tail. But sometimes it will just say 'sidecut radius' in metres.**

BOOT ANATOMY

1 Liner
2 Power strap
3 Flex/lean adjust
4 Cuff/cant adjust
5 Heel flange
6 Toe flange

Child's boot

Lady's boot

Your ski boots are probably the most important link in the chain. They support your ankles, protect your shins, and deliver your intent to the skis. For this reason it's very important that they fit correctly. If they are too tight, they will hurt your feet a lot in the course of a long day on the hill. If they are too loose you won't have the desired degree of control, or of safety.

A good ski shop will have some clever technology to analyse your gait and adjust new boots for pronation or supination, as well as all the other adjustments that can be made for optimum performance. Most modern boots have thermally moulded liners, which means that you put them on hot and they morph to fit your feet permanently. There are some types of liners that allow you to do this yourself at home the first time. Clearly, therefore, it's important to use the kind of socks you will typically wear for skiing, when fitting boots. Hire boots don't offer you this luxury. You select your size off the shelf and check they feel OK in the shop, and that's the end of the fitting process. The sock thing still stands, though...

Ski boots seem impossibly stiff, when you handle them, but in fact flex is important. It just has to be exactly the right amount of flex. Once you are wearing them you will find that the ankle, in particular, can bend quite a bit.

Here you can see the cam clips that close the boot, and the walk/ride switch that releases/locks the boot and cuff.

Ski poles, sticks or batons are the one bit of skiing hardware that is blessedly simple (and cheap), but they do come in many forms. The pole bit itself is generally constant, a lightweight tapered tube made from aluminium or carbon fibre, sometimes shaped slightly to suit a specific discipline. Racing poles for instance, are curved to fit around the body when tucked. But there are a multitude of 'basket' designs available depending on the type of skiing.

⬆ **The original style of twin-pole basket**

⬆ **The cut out segement allows you to clip two poles together for ease of carrying.**

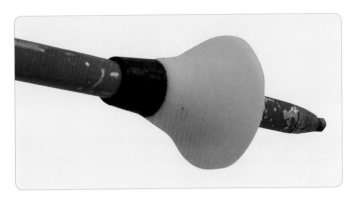

⇧ **Aerodynamic racing basket**

⇧ **A cross-country pole basket**

⇧ **A different kind of cross-country/touring basket**

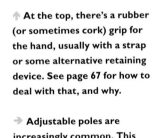

⇧ **A larger basket for deeper snow and backcountry touring**

⇧ **At the top, there's a rubber (or sometimes cork) grip for the hand, usually with a strap or some alternative retaining device. See page 67 for how to deal with that, and why.**

➡ **Adjustable poles are increasingly common. This can save the hire shop holding too many sizes, and they are also popular for adventure or backcountry skiing. For instance, you might want to make the pole longer for hiking up, and then shorten it again for the descent.**

⇧ **The normal length of poles for downhill skiing is such that, when planted in the snow by your toes, your forearms will be horizontal when gripping the handles. To check this out in the shop, where there is no snow, it's best to hold them upside down and grip the stem below the basket.**

However, cross-country poles are often longer, for pushing with, and some aggressive telemarkers use shorter poles because of the lower body position.

Poles are relatively fragile, by virtue of their light weight. Try not to sit on them, fall on them, or shut them in doors.

BRAKES

When your alpine bindings do release, the brake levers come down to ensure your skis don't head on down without you if they land right side up. These levers are also used to clip the skis together so you can carry them.

ANTI-FRICTION DEVICE (AFD)

AFD is a serious-sounding acronym for a slippy bit that solves a binding release problem. Some time ago, ski designers were busy patting themselves on that back for inventing the modern binding and saving people from breaking their legs every five minutes, and then they discovered that sometimes the boots grip or get iced into position. So most skis now have some device to assist twist and rotation, designed to minimise the friction between binding and boot during lateral release. The purpose of the AFD is to let the boot roll or slide sideways more easily during an incident.

ELASTIC MOVEMENT

To reduce the likelihood of the skis falling off prematurely, bindings allow a certain amount of elastic travel for vertical and lateral movements before releasing the boot. This elastic movement in your bindings is also designed to provide substantial shock absorption during vibrations and bumps. Some bindings are designed to provide more elastic movement than others – a racer, for instance, doesn't need everything to be wobbling about.

ALPINE TOURING SKI BINDINGS

These allow the skier to lift their heel to ascend the mountain and lock it down for descents. Touring bindings are specifically for skiers who ski the backcountry. Because an alpine touring binding must function in two modes (ascent and descent), its design is relatively complex compared to a traditional alpine binding.

TELEMARK SKI BINDINGS

Telemark bindings can only be used with special telemark boots. They are designed to bend at the bellows behind the toes to allow the heel to lift, so you can both hike forwards and upwards, and make the iconic 'soul turn'.

RELEASE FORCE SETTING (DIN)

DIN, short for Deutsches Institut für Normung (German Institute for Standards), is the worldwide system for release settings on ski bindings. The DIN should be properly set by a technician, based on your stated weight, height and ability level, when you buy or hire a pair of skis. The idea is that the skis will pop off in a crash to reduce the chances of injury, but not pop off when you are cranking that big stivot turn or landing a double back flip! Nordic skis do not have DIN release technology because the free heel (arguably) makes injury less likely.

⬇ **This photo shows the AFD (anti-friction device) and the DIN gauge.**

⬆ **Telemark boot with hinged toe section.**

SKI BOOT WEAR

Boots can be maintained and repaired. Buckles, in particular, may break and need replacing. But when the toe and heel flange are excessively worn, this will affect the safety of the binding functionality, and it's time to replace the boots.

MAINTAINING SKI BINDINGS

Unless otherwise specified by the manufacturer, ski bindings are designed to be maintenance free. However, manufacturers normally recommend that you have your bindings inspected by a professional before the start of each season.

KEEP BINDINGS FREE OF GRIT, CORROSION, SALT ETC.

Don't wash or clean your bindings with strong soap or solvents, as you may remove factory lubricants, which are essential for proper operation and function. Always store your skis and bindings in a dry place and don't leave them wet for long periods.

HIRE OR BUY?

The decision whether to hire skis or buy them is a tricky one, and mainly it depends on how often you ski. There are some other considerations. For some people it's a financial decision, and in that instance there definitely is a break-even point based on usage. But some people just like owning stuff. Some people really don't like the idea of wearing boots that hundreds of people have worn before. Most boots these days are custom fitted to the skier's feet, and that doesn't happen with hire boots.

You can hire your equipment in your home place, and then take it with you on holiday, but I've never understood why anyone would do this. Every ski resort has multiple ski shops, most of which make most of their money from hiring skis. Don't be fobbed off with something you aren't happy with. If something isn't working out for you, you can take it back to the store and change it.

RENTING EQUIPMENT

Pros:
- You don't have any maintenance to deal with. Pick up your skis waxed and sharp, and drop them off at the end of your stay. Done.
- You don't have to transport your skis, boots and poles. All heavy and cumbersome kit, that can cost extra to fly and is hassle if you drive.
- You can choose new equipment every time allowing you to use the latest gear.
- You can hire skis that suit the conditions. Snowed overnight? Pop in and exchange your all-mountain skis for fat powder-specific ones. Terrible visibility or piste conditions? Get some cross-country skis and do that instead.
- Often ski hire shops have lockers where you can leave equipment overnight to avoid carrying it back to your accommodation. You can stroll down there in your trainers in the morning. Bonus!

Cons:
- You may be offered poor quality or damaged equipment, especially if you're a beginner.
- Long queues in the shop, especially during school holidays.
- Each time you go skiing, you have to get used to something new. This is OK if you go once a year, as you probably won't remember!

BUYING EQUIPMENT

Pros:
- No messing around in ski hire shops.
- You choose the kit you want and have it set up exactly for you.
- You don't have to wear pre-used boots.
- You learn more quickly.

Cons:
- You have to transport heavy equipment.
- Cost or time invested in servicing the kit.
- You need to have somewhere at home to store equipment.
- You'll spend money not only buying the kit, but every time you want to change it or upgrade.
- If you buy one set of kit, it'll quickly be followed by others for different conditions.
- If you have a technical problem during your stay, it'll be expensive to sort it out in resort.

Of course, the hire/buy decision isn't limited to an entire set of gear. You could buy boots and hire the rest. Worth thinking about.

The different types of skiing are illustrated on pages 10 to 11. Whether you're hiring or buying, you need to know what type of skiing you are planning to do. Most in-resort hire shops are 90% alpine skiing orientated. If you walk in and say 'I want to hire some skis', they'll presume that you want alpine. They'll also ask your weight and skiing ability. Be honest, because as well as determining the best size of ski, this affects the DIN setting of the binding, which is a massive safety issue.

PHOTOGRAPHING YOUR ADVENTURE

In these days of social media, it's increasingly important to many of us to share (show off) images of our adventures with friends and family, but disappointingly, our skiing holiday photos often fall short of the awesomeness that every skier feels they're displaying on the slopes, and we're often reduced to a handful of posed shots of a row of slightly sheepish people in front of a mountain. Like any kind of photography, the solution is just a few simple techniques and the right equipment, and luckily in the case of good skiing weather, the right equipment is almost any camera.

That's right – one of the common frustrations of actual professional skiing photographers is that on a good day, a phone or a compact camera can often capture amazing images. And currently, it seems half the people on the slopes have some sort of personal action camera permanently fixed to some part of their anatomy!

The reason that it's possible to take fantastic, professional-looking ski photos with the most mundane cameras is that the snow hill environment is very bright when the weather is good. This means that the camera can shoot the picture at a high shutter speed, which

↑ **Downhill action is often best shot looking uphill. Get as low as you can, lying down if possible, and try to have some sort of horizon in the shot that adds a sense of perspective.**

↓ **Looking across the piste is often good with a stationary skier. It's best to have a background, not just snow or sky, and again a diagonal to give some impression of slope.**

is a good thing for action photography as it captures sharp images of moving subjects. It also means that automatic cameras default to quite a small aperture, so that objects near and far can be in focus at the same time. This doesn't make for artistic photos, but it's a bonus when it's difficult to ensure the camera focuses where you wanted it to.

SAFETY – IT'S BEST TO STOP AND TAKE PHOTOS FROM A SAFE LOCATION IN CLEAR VIEW AT THE SIDE OF THE PISTE. TRYING TO TAKE PHOTOS WHILE YOU ARE SKIING DOWNHILL IS A BIG CAUSE OF CRASHES. AND BAD PHOTOS...

The most common way to take a photo of someone skiing is to stop and shoot uphill as they ski down towards you. Unfortunately, this rarely gives the impression of speed and steepness that the skier was actually feeling. The resulting photo is usually of someone in the middle of some whiteness, with no sense of location or gradient. A better way is to shoot looking down on the skier, or get really low (maybe even lie down) and shoot up. Photos with a fairly low horizon line behind the subject work well, whether looking upwards or across. See the examples on this page.

There are a few classic technical problems that apply to most types of photographic equipment in the snow, so let's take a look at those before we examine specific bits of kit.

BATTERY LIFE

The life of all types of battery is dramatically reduced in the cold. When I say dramatically, I'm not being 'dramatic' – it can result in a phone that normally lasts all day working for about an hour. The answer is to keep the camera warm inside layers of clothing, and only get it out when needed. An outside pocket might be at -5°C, whereas an inside one will be at 30°C – warmer than your home, probably. The other solution, if you are shooting a lot, is spare batteries. These should also be kept warm, of course.

CONDENSATION

When your camera is taken from a warm environment to a very cold one, any moisture held in the warm(ish) air inside it tends to condense, leaving water droplets in all sorts of unwelcome places but most particularly on the inside of the lens. It's very irritating.

The problem is particularly noticeable with action cameras like the one shown – assemble the case indoors and then take it somewhere cold, and this is the result. But equally, it can happen with most types of camera that you let air in and out of. SLRs with interchangeable lenses, for instance. The answer is to assemble everything somewhere fairly cold.

WHITE BALANCE (COLOUR TEMPERATURE)

Many cameras have an auto white balance setting, which does an acceptable job in most situations, but the snowy environment throws up some special problems. First of all, everything is white, so the camera struggles to find an average (grey) area to calibrate from. Secondly, there is a lot of UV light in the mountains, and although this is invisible to the naked eye, it can give camera images a weird blue/purple tint. If you can use a UV filter (either physical or electronic), that helps. If you can figure out how to set your camera's white balance manually, either to a snow setting or by calibrating off a suitable surface, that helps even more.

LCD SCREENS

Most phones and dedicated cameras use an LCD display to show you what you are shooting. This is often difficult to see properly in a super-bright environment, and glare or UV often add to your problems. If you can stop in the shade to take the photo, it helps. Also, consider that certain types of eyewear make it harder to see the screen – try with and without your goggles or shades.

TYPES OF CAMERA

Phones

Using your phone as a camera is convenient and increasingly effective. You only have to carry one device, and you can upload images to social media with ease. The downside of the phone is that you usually don't have much control over the settings (see above) and it is sometimes difficult to see what you are shooting.

⬇ Many phones are touchscreen these days, and don't work well (or at all) if you are using gloves. Pull off your gloves, and you may have sweaty fingers, which don't work accurately on the screen, and become cold or frozen quickly when exposed. I like to wear these touchscreen compatible thin gloves inside a waterproof outer glove or mitten. Attach the outer to yourself with a leash and you may save yourself some juggling action too!

⬇ If you do end up juggling and dropping your phone, it can embed itself without trace in the snow. While it is still on, you can zero in on it with your avalanche transceiver if you can get within a metre or two. It's good practice, too!

Compact

Modern compact cameras take awesome pictures on auto settings, but think about using the manual features and sport settings as well!

Gopro-type cameras

The personal action camera is very popular in extreme sports, but it's

⬇ **The digital SLR is the pinnacle of sports photography, but most people don't want to risk one on the hill. A proper camera bag is worth having!**

generally much better for filming yourself than anything else. Subjects more than a metre or two away will look very distant and small. If you are shooting video, consider a higher than normal frame rate so that slow motion can be achieved at a higher quality. Many people wear them on their person to give a point-of-view (POV) feel. The most popular mounting is on the helmet, but this gives a very jerky end result unless you are very professional at aiming your head. For skiing a chest mount is more stable. It can also be very versatile to mount it on one of your sticks as shown in the photo.

HOW IT WORKS AT THE HILL

⬆ **There will be lots of hire shops. You can sometimes get a discount by booking online before you arrive.**

⬆ **Most resorts have a free bus that drives round and round so that you don't have to walk from your hotel to the hill.**

No one ever tells you this stuff. Luckily nearly all ski resorts work the same way so you can wise up pretty easily and avoid spending your first week stumbling about in ski boots wondering what's what! Read on.

To use the ski lifts you need to buy a ski pass. This will normally be from an office or counter near the car park or lifts, but not at the lift itself, so don't join the big giant queue without one! You can get one for the day, or just a half day, or for multiple days or weeks. It usually works out cheaper the more time you buy. For cross-country skiing and touring you usually don't need to buy a pass just to be on the hill per se, but you won't be able to use the lifts. Until recently the ski pass was a ticket that you had to show to the lift attendant. Later it became a card you placed in a slot to release the gate or turnstile to the lift, so the attendant didn't need to check your pass. Nowadays, almost all resorts use electronic cards that you can leave in your pocket at all times. They are detected automatically by a sensor as you approach the turnstile, which releases to let you through. This system provides the resort with

valuable data about skier behaviours and usage patterns so that they can refine their service.

It is usual now for the resort to take your photo while selling you the lift pass, and this photo will be included in the data on the card. When you go through the turnstile to use the lift, your face will flash up on the attendant's computer screen. This is a fraud prevention measure. You can't share your pass with someone else. It also prevents people living in the resort from purchasing cheaper, locals-only season passes and then renting them out to guests, for instance.

The place that you can buy these lift tickets is usually right next to the lowest lift that is used to access the mountain. You can sometimes buy them in other places, for instance the tourist office, your hotel or tour guide, or even in the ski shop when you collect equipment, and this can save queuing on busy days.

There is usually a big car park close to the lowest lifts, too. The norm for European resorts is for this parking to be free, but it isn't always. Make sure. If you drive to the lifts you can put your ski boots on near to the hill, but if you are walking there from your hotel, you may have to walk in your boots. Some resorts have lockers where you can put a pair of shoes, but it's not all that common. So, you could take a backpack and carry a pair of trainers around all day so that you don't have to walk to and from the hill in your boots. Or just tough it out and learn to walk in ski boots. It's a thing worth thinking about, though. Very few people find it easy to walk in ski boots, even with the clips undone, so most don't undertake any distance. It's not too bad on snow, but on the pavement it's a nightmare. If you see someone doing it effortlessly, it's probably an instructor or some other sort of professional. Or a telemarker, since they are all naturally imbued with god-like athleticism. I'm joking (I'm a telemarker), telemark boots look very similar to normal ski boots but they're a fair bit easier to walk in.

SKI RACKS, SECURITY ETC.

When you are up the hill, you will see racks outside the mountain bars and restaurants for your skis. No one locks their equipment to these. Everyone up on the mountain already has a set of skis on, and has paid for an expensive lift ticket. So while it's theoretically possible for someone of a criminal persuasion to go up and steal skis, it doesn't really happen. Down at the bottom of the mountain, though, it's a different story. Thieves can and do simply stroll by and lift people's kit. Some establishments have their own locking system for your skis, but it's as well to carry your own lock.

A typical skier will wear a snowproof jacket over a warm fleece or other insulating layer, snowproof trousers designed to connect with ski boots, and a warm hat.

As well as your skis, boots and poles, you should at this stage be wearing 'suitable' clothing. I love this part. There is a wider variety of wardrobe strategies than there used to be a few years ago, so you'll see a lot of different clothing choices on the hill, and it's a minefield to choose an outfit. My advice is, mix and match from whichever of the following seems to fit your kind of skiing.

Most beginners start out with some ski trousers or salopettes that are snowproof and a bit padded, and a jacket that's, you guessed it, snowproof and a bit padded. This is suitable for the majority of different ski resort activities, although perhaps not for the backcountry. There are, however, a number of other options.

LEGWEAR OPTIONS

I'm going to go out on a limb (oh, I'm so funny) and suggest that generally people wear the same trousers/pants irrespective of the conditions. On a cold day you might wear more underneath, but you only need one pair of trousers (for each skiing discipline, at any rate).

However... I always like to own/take two pairs of ski pants on a trip. Just in case I forget to dry them overnight, or leave them in a car or on a balcony to freeze. A warm, padded pair and a waterproof shell pair works for me – not much extra weight or bulk, and useful to have options depending on the weather, too. Waterproof shell pants (Gore-Tex or similar) have no insulation value or padding value, but total dryness value.

Stretch pants make a lot of sense and look good if you have great legs and bum. They have the advantage of being low drag in deep powder, and the disadvantage that you can't add underlayers very well on colder days. They also lack the waterproofness and versatility for the backcountry or for bad conditions.

➡ **Padded ski pants or salopettes (bib pants) are the most common choice for skiers. They can be quite fitted, or baggy, but the key benefit is that they are warm and dry in most conditions, and a little padding can't hurt!**

⬇ **Lycra if you are a cross-country nut or a racer, yes. Otherwise, no...**

⬇ **A lot of ski trousers now come with braces/suspenders, and there's a fashion, particularly among freeskiers, for skiing with them hanging and wearing a belt instead. It's quite dangerous, particularly on lifts.**

DOWN JACKET

FLEECE

WHAT TO WEAR ON TOP

Jackets are a bit more of a mixed bag. Depending on the weather, I might go out wearing just a hoodie or sweater, or one of a variety of different jackets.

Snowproof shells

Some shell garments are snowproof, but not really waterproof. Cotton or microfibre, or softshell garments fall into this category. They are more breathable than even the most breathable of waterproof garments, but ultimately no fun if you get rained on. I will make specific mention of the Pertex/pile type combo, because it is a favourite with adventure skiers and mountain rescue teams the world over. It's a great garment to own, and brilliant climate control on 90% of days, but again in actual wet and freezing conditions, you'll wish you had a waterproof jacket.

Insulated ski jacket

The padded or insulated ski jacket used to be the standard fare, and it still works well on most days. However, it's not properly waterproof, and it's sometimes too hot, because you can't un-insulate it! But it's ideal for the holiday skier who wants to keep things simple.

Fleece

Synthetic fleece is a staple outdoor clothing, and it's the perfect mid-layer to wear under your snow or waterproof shells. However, it's not great to wear as an outer layer, even if the weather is fine, because snow seems magnetically attracted to it, and sticks...

Down jacket

Natural or synthetic down filled, these are the warmest garments known to man or woman. They are also quite snowproof, but they let us down (sorry...) in wet conditions and they are prone to damage/tearing from sharp equipment, or trees. They are light and pack down (again, really?) very small, however, so they can be a good thing to carry as extra insulation.

Waterproof shells

More and more people now use a waterproof and breathable outer shell (Gore-Tex is but one example) in combination with a layering system (thermals, fleece or wool jumper). They really are the best choice for variable conditions, because you are safe from rain or wet snow, and powder, and you can unzip or vent in hot conditions, or take it off completely.

ONE-PIECE SKI SUITS

One-piece suits were very popular in the seventies, and both classic and modern incarnations can still be seen today. Opinions are divided about them on the fashion front, but they do present some very clear advantages and disadvantages that we can consider.

The ski suit doesn't have a gap in the middle, which means that no matter what befalls you, there won't be snow getting in, or a cold back on the lift chair. However, they lack the versatility to strip off in warm weather or to make adjustments on the fly. You can unzip the front a bit, or open any vents there may be, and that's about it. It's also a bulky piece of kit that doesn't really double up as

WATERPROOF
SHELL

ONE-PIECE SKI SUIT

anything else, so you still need to take another jacket to wear in the evenings. It's up to you to decide whether the advantages outweigh these limitations.

EVERYDAY CLOTHES

It wouldn't be right to finish this part of the book without mentioning those skiers who go out on the slopes wearing their everyday clothes.

It's easy to criticise – jeans, for instance, are not really the best choice for outdoor sportswear, but you must realise that some people are very unlikely to fall, and if the weather is nice, it's an acceptable solution (or fashion choice) for some expert skiers. Cross-country skiers, too, sometimes eschew technical sports clothing in favour of just wearing ordinary clothes. It isn't the best decision for everyone. Accidents can happen, and weather can change. But it makes for a bit of variety.

JEANS

GLOVES

Choice of gloves is really important. They do the essential and obvious job of keeping your hands warm, but they also protect you in the event of a fall. Depending what kind of skiing you do, there are a number of options that you might want to consider.

⬆ **Fleece gloves are good as liners or for cross-country, but not enough for downhill skiing.**

⬇ **I like to wear woollen gloves under mitts. They get trashed easily on their own. These ones have a touchscreen compatible feature.**

⬆ **Neoprene gloves are warm and water resistant but get sweaty.**

⬇ **These are insulated and reinforced gloves, pretty much the top of the line and great if you carry your skis a lot.**

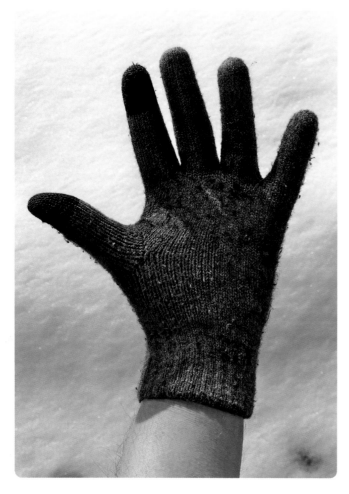

⬇ **Mittens are not particularly fashionable, but the warmest solution, especially with thinner gloves as liners.**

SOCKS

New skiers always think of socks as deserving more attention than most other pieces of clothing or personal equipment, but I don't really agree. You can spend a lot of money on special, technical ski socks, and usually they wear out pretty quickly. That last part is not, perhaps, surprising. Back in the day, when people used wooden skis and wore leather walking/hiking boots for skiing in, it was essential to wear big, thick woollen socks to keep the feet and lower legs warm in freezing conditions. Wool is also excellent when wet, and dries out again quickly. Hence it continues to be a good choice for skiing. Nowadays, however, there are many synthetic sock fabrics, and most are suitable for skiing. Natural cotton is perhaps the only type of sock I'd specifically avoid, because it's not very stretchy and it's rubbish when wet.

Modern ski boots are very technical and insulated, so you don't need thick socks to keep warm. Thickness doesn't give you extra padding, either. It just makes your feet less stable in the boots, which should fit perfectly to your foot shape. However, you might wear different footwear to walk to the hill, or around the house/hotel, so think about that socks-wise. But for actual skiing, thin socks are fine. I don't

⬇ **It's good if your socks come up to the top of your boot.**

understand super-techy socks that have padding in particular areas. If your boot fits, these areas will just cause pressure.

If your boots are not thermoformed to fit your feet (you wear hire boots, for instance), then you might want a selection of socks thick and thin, so that you can fine-tune the perfect fit. It's easier to take off one pair of socks when your boots start to feel too tight, than it is to take the boots back to the shop and get the next size up (that's probably too big)!

The thing to check is that your socks are stretchy enough to fit your feet perfectly with no folds or rucks, but not sooooo stretchy that they distort and cause such things once they're in the boot. They should be tall enough that they don't end halfway up the boot, but somewhere above the power strap.

The really important thing about socks is to make sure each and every time you put them on that there are no burrs or pilling inside or out. The tiniest little lump or bump will feel like a pea in your boot, and all too soon turn to a burning sensation and a blister. Ruins your day. So inspect socks carefully, and replace when needed. Avoid ribbed or other textured socks for the same reason.

UNDERGARMENTS/THERMALS – AND DO WE NEED THEM?

Underwear is generally a good idea, or so I was always told. Thermals are another matter. It depends on the climate and your level of activity, of course, but people are usually surprised that they get too hot when they are out skiing. If you get much too hot, you will sweat inside your waterproof clothes and then get wet, clammy and cold. So, it's good to wear thermals, as long as they aren't crazy hot. A thin, technical base layer keeps you safe from overheating and manages perspiration best. It can also prevent fatigue or injury by applying a bit of muscle compression. It doesn't make you invincible, though, however much you may feel like a superhero when you put it on!

FINALLY, AND DESERVING OF A BIT OF OUR TIME – NECKWEAR

There are many different types of scarf or face mask, but choose something that is comfortable whether worn over the face or just to keep the neck warm. Scarves made from cotton, fleece or wool are not suitable if it's snowing or you're going to be brave, because they get wet or snowy and then they aren't comfy. Lycra or similar on the outside lets snow and moisture slide off, even if the inside is fleecy and warm. If you put your goggles on over your scarf they tend to steam up, because your breath escapes up and over your cheekbones, unless there are breathing holes to let it out in the normal way.

← **Sunglasses may be more comfortable for cross-country skiing and touring, but it would be sensible to take them off for a fast descent.**

WHY WEAR EYE PROTECTION?

There are many good reasons. In the mountains, the air is thinner and filters less ultraviolet (UV) light. The sun's reflection on snow is also bright and more intense. Wind can make your eyes teary and sore. And ice crystals can get into your eyes, especially when skiing fast. Twigs and branches will hit your eyes when skiing through the trees.

Tip: If you're not wearing a helmet, don't put your goggles on top of your head. Warm air from your scalp is saturated with perspiration, and goggles sitting on the head will trap this moisture. You'll be struggling to clear your lenses for the rest of the day!

UV PROTECTION

Virtually all modern goggles offer 100% UV protection from all three types of ultraviolet rays (UVA, UVB and UVC). Remember that even when it is cloudy, UV rays are reflected off the snow.

Double lenses: Found on most goggles since they do not fog as easily as single-layered lenses, but be sure that the two layers are sealed properly. This creates a thermal barrier (like double glazing) that is more resistant to fogging. An anti-fog coating (see below) will help ward off fogging.

Anti-fog coatings: Integrated into most mid- to high-end goggle lenses to help deter fogging. The coating is on the inside of the inside lens. For this reason you should never wipe clean the inside of your goggles. The coating can be quite fragile and get scratched, even with a soft cloth, and especially in the presence of microscopic ice crystals. If the inside does steam up, stop skiing and try to dry it out with sunlight or other heat, rather than wiping it.

Vents: The top, sides and bottom of goggles are the keys to help control fogging. Wider vents generally create better ventilating airflow than smaller venting holes. On the other hand your face may get cold, particularly in extreme conditions. Some goggle designs feature adjustable vents.

LENS COLOUR

OK, here we go with a subject that is the cause of a great deal of frustration to me. Despite the fact that there are now a number of online resources that explain quite well the advantages and disadvantages of different lens colours in the snow, there is an important part of the message that is not getting across. Most retailers at home (outside of ski regions) will want to sell you an 'all-round' lens, which seems like a very good idea until you realise that these goggles are pretty poor in all conditions. This is the reason that people who go on holiday to ski usually turn up with a very expensive pair of

Most readers will be unaware that a mountain dweller uses many different types of eye protection, depending on the circumstances and the conditions.

You will see many skiers wearing sunglasses on the slopes instead of goggles. I don't recommend this, for downhill skiing at any rate. Even robust sports sunglasses have a lot of potential for injuring the wearer in the event of a fall or other accident. Even if they don't break or pop a lens out and cut your face, the ends of the arms of the sunglasses can still stab you. It just isn't worth the risk, when goggles provide superior performance in all areas apart from the (admittedly important) looking hot department!

↓ **Buy über-cheap goggles at your peril!**

is to own several different goggles, and think about the weather before you go out. If it looks likely to change, maybe consider taking a second pair to deal with the possible problems when the clouds come in, or blow away!

🔻 **Mirrored lenses are not necessary to cut out light, but more of a fashion statement. They scratch on the outside more easily than ordinary tinted lenses, so beware!**

⬆ **Skiing quickly on a grey, overcast day requires suitable light-coloured goggles to bring out the details in the terrain.**

goggles with an all-round lens, whereas people who live and/or work in the snow tend to own several sets of less-fashionable eyewear, with various colours of lenses for different conditions.

I made the same mistake when I lived in the UK and went on skiing holidays. I could never understand how locals seemed to be able to ski perfectly well in fog, or flat light, or high glare conditions when I couldn't see a damn thing! When I moved to live in the Alps, a kindly shopkeeper explained the whole situation to me, and also sold me goggles that were one fifth the price of the 'cool' ones back home, despite being technically very good quality.

So here are the benefits of different lens colour choices:

Yellow	**Enhances visual acuity, shadows and depth perception. Best in flat light or fog/cloud.**
Gold	**Enhances shadow perception and contrast. Best all-round lens.**
Orange	**Enhances shadow perception. Moderate fog or cloud.**
Brown	**Increases contrast. Bright conditions.**
Grey	**Maintains true colour. Bright sun.**
Rose	**Increases depth perception. Flat light conditions, often sold as an all-round lens.**
Rose/Bronze	**Increases contrast and depth perception. Fog or low/dark cloud.**
Clear	**Allows in most light. Falling snow conditions, sunset, night.**

It is sometimes possible to purchase goggles that have interchangeable lenses, so that you can easily carry a number of different options in your pocket. This is great if you can find some. Otherwise, the best thing to do

➡ **The spherical lens is curved in both planes and gives a less distorted view but is more expensive.**

HELMETS AND OTHER PROTECTION

More and more skiers are now wearing helmets, at least for downhill skiing. There is still a minority who have never worn one, and don't see the need to, but more and more people are adopting the lid as their standard wear, influenced by its increasing acceptance and no doubt a number of celebrity incidents in the media. All children now wear helmets to ski, and as these little ones grow up, they become the adults who never had any reason not to.

Whether or not helmets prevent head injuries is not scientifically proven, partly because of the ever-changing research landscape of their recent introduction, and partly because there is some implication that wearing a helmet makes you braver/more foolhardy. But it doesn't need to be proved. What is clear is that the use of a suitable helmet minimises the severity of any head impact injury. When we look at this statement in the context of the negatives associated with helmet use, it becomes a bit of a no-brainer. If you'll pardon the expression...

Positive arguments for helmet use (as opposed to the typical woolly hat):
- Minimise the damage caused by head impact.
- Stop your goggles misting when you put them up.
- Keep your head dry in snowfall and powder.
- Better control over warmth/hearing and all-important earphones.

Negative arguments for helmets:
- You might look a bit of a numpty – this is inadmissible, since 80% of US skiers and 50% of Europeans are using them, although you potentially look a bit funny wearing a helmet at a restaurant, so...
- You might need to take a hat with you to wear while sitting out on the terrace – no problem, you can use it to protect the sunglasses you'll be carrying for the same reason!

So I think we can surmise from my extremely scientific comparison above, that you should probably wear a helmet.

Here are a few things to think about.

⬇ **Make sure that the helmet can be adjusted to sit comfortably on your head, without exposing your ears or forehead, and without moving around unduly.**

Liner – liners are made for comfort as well as protection and are often removable for washing/drying.

Chin strap – with padding and adjustment for angle as well as length.

Earpieces – these keep the ears warm (and in-ear headphones in) better than a beanie.

➡ **Make sure your helmet works with your goggles. Or vice versa. The strap will need to go around the helmet and that's bigger than your head.**

⬇ **There is usually a retaining point at the back to locate the goggle strap.**

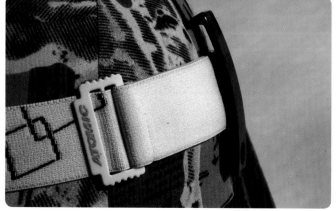

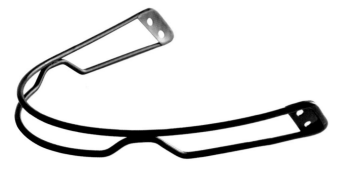

⬆ **Chinguards are used by racers because they get hit by poles. A lot.**

It is a good idea to replace your helmet regularly. Three seasons is probably the safe maximum for a plastic helmet. Other materials may vary so consult the manufacturer.

OTHER IMPACT PROTECTION

It's hard to know where to stop with protective equipment. The first piece that I bought was a pair of armoured shorts, purchased after an undignified and extremely painful landing. I've never had that injury again, whether wearing the shorts or not, but I have in the meantime suffered shoulder, back, knee, wrist and nose injuries on more than one occasion each. Should I buy the kit for those too? I'll end up going skiing looking like Robocop!

To my mind, the main reason to wear serious protection is to moderate the threat to a pre-existing weakness, or when the activity is likely to result in a serious risk of injury. So, if you have weak knees, wear a knee brace. If you have a tendency to fall on your hands, wrist support. If wearing too much reduces your enjoyment of skiing, act on that. If not being protected ruins your day through anxiety, suit up!

What I've observed in myself and others is a sort of stable-door phenomenon, wherein we claim that protection is too expensive and encumbering, until we hurt ourselves, and then we buy something to defend that one area, continuing to leave the other body parts unprotected. There is a serious lack of logic to this strategy, but equally you can't go skiing on the bunny slope in full body armour.

⬆ **Padded protective shorts.**

⬆ **Protective vest.**　　⬆ **Protective back plate.**

➡ **Most skiing body armour uses a scale-like design to allow flexibility while preventing over-extension.**

⬆ **Some people, racers in particular, wear full body protection.**

LEARNING TO SKI

To learn how to ski, you are going to need a ski instructor. You can go to 'Ski School' or have one-to-one tuition according to your inclination and your budget, but instruction you will undoubtedly require. Even once you can ski, you'll benefit from taking regular lessons in order to keep improving and to iron out bad habits that you may have acquired along the way. Even the best skiers in the world regularly work with coaches in order to fine-tune their performance, so there's no shame in doing this at all.

I really don't recommend that you get a friend or family member to teach you to ski, unless they are a professional. Equally, while you're out practising with your friends when ski school is over, do take any suggestions that your friends make with a pinch of salt. Ski instructors really do know best. This is despite the fact that they are usually local farmboys/girls who, for a brief few months each year, get to wear a smart uniform and become, inexplicably, irresistible to the opposite sex and, in many cases, the same sex. That's because they are awesome skiers, and by virtue of the fact that they very quickly become great at showing people how to have a good time. They are fortunate in this, because skiing itself is incredibly cool, exciting and good fun. I don't imagine that teaching people how to fillet fish or change a bicycle chain is anything like such a good social lubricant.

AM I GOING TO FALL OVER?

That depends on how experienced you are, but not in the way you might imagine. Contrary to the advice that I find in many books about skiing, I really don't think there is any good reason for beginners to fall over. There's nothing to be gained from falling over, apart from practice at getting back up again. However, if you are an experienced and skilful skier, and you never fall down, then I have to ask whether you are really pushing yourself. If you try to improve and push your personal limits, it's always going to get away from you sometimes!

If you are a beginner, however, you should not have to fall over. If you do, then you are trying to progress too quickly through the drills, or the terrain is too difficult for what you have already learned. Go back a few stages and then re-cover old ground.

AM I GOING TO HURT MYSELF?

You shouldn't injure yourself while skiing, despite some of the stereotypical images of people returning from ski trips in plaster which abound, particularly in the UK. Equipment and training have come a long way since those ideas were ubiquitous. Adhere to the drills this

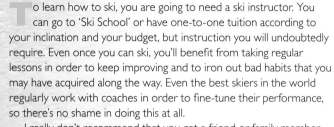

DID YOU KNOW?

Q. What's the difference between God and a ski instructor?
A. God doesn't think he's a ski instructor.

book and your instructor give you, and the fitness and preparation sections of the book, and you should be able to laugh off any little bumps and tumbles.

IS IT DIFFICULT TO LEARN?

No. Standing up at all is pretty difficult, and walking is an incredibly complex skill. It took you the first couple of years of your life, practising all day every day, to become competent at those two activities, and that was while you were at the peak of your ability to learn. You can pick up skiing in a matter of days, however – it's just a few additional concepts to bolt onto your existing skills. In fact, in places where it's snowy all winter and there are hills, most three year olds can ski perfectly well. How hard can it be?

IS IT AS EASY AS IT LOOKS, THOUGH?

Ah, well no it isn't. Competent skiers make it look very easy, and then when you try to emulate them, nothing seems to work the way you expected. And that's why you need a ski instructor, as well as the concepts that are described in this book. Because while it is just a few extra bits and pieces to add to your existing repertoire, they are all quite counter-intuitive. For instance, you may read/hear about 'foot steering'. When a beginner is put on skis for the first time they can be forgiven for imagining that they will simply be able to turn the skis with their feet to point in the direction that they want to go. Nothing could be further from the truth. It doesn't work at all.

You will definitely find it physically demanding at first, trying to do all these unfamiliar actions, and very probably for much longer than

you are used to exercising any other way. Have a look at the section on fitness training (page 54) to try to head this problem off in advance.

A skier is a bit like a racing car. Aerodynamics aside, the only thing that matters is the forces that are acting upon the area(s) in contact with the ground (the skis/tyres), and everything that you do should be in consideration of that fact. However, a skier is more like a dancer. As a wise man once said to me, the dance does not take place on the ground. It takes place in the air. So it is what you do with the entire body that determines the forces that act on the snow, dance floor, or racetrack.

WAXING AND SERVICING YOUR SKIS

If you use hire skis, there's no real need for you to read this bit. If you have your own skis, you should be aware of the basic principles, and you can decide whether to delegate ski maintenance to your local ski technician, or do it yourself to save money and risk incurring the wrath of whoever handles your domestic arrangements.

Wax does two things. It makes the sole or base of the ski slide correctly on the snow, and it also seals it, preventing moisture from waterlogging the core and rusting the edges from the inside. A correctly waxed ski does not look as if it is coated in wax, particularly, but the base will probably look dry and powdery if it needs waxing. The way most people notice that they need wax, however, is that the skis suddenly seem a bit slow.

How wax works is very counter-intuitive. Far from making the ski more slippery, it actually makes it slightly grippy. This, in turn, causes some friction, which heats and melts the tips of the snow crystals, giving us a lubricated surface to slide on. Unfortunately, no one has yet created a wax that does this across all ranges of snow temperatures and air humidity. So sometimes, you find that your freshly waxed skis just don't want to slide. Almost as if the snow has become sticky. Or turned into sand.

For this reason, most ski shops sell different temperature waxes. A little forethought, and you can wax up with the right product for the range of snow temperatures you can expect the next day. The hire company probably don't do this, so what they have put on a set of skis is anybody's guess.

FILLING

Any deep gouges should be filled before edging and waxing. You can do this with a plastic (P-tex) material, as shown here.

← **You can light the P-tex with a flame, or melt it with a hot iron.**

↓ **Drip the P-tex into the gouge and then iron it in or wait for it to cool. Sand it with fine abrasive paper wrapped around a cork block.**

EDGING

Before waxing your skis you should tune the metal edges. You can buy an inexpensive tool to help with this, and it's not worth skimping and trying to use something else, because you'll risk irrevocable damage to the rails. A good tip is to run a felt tip pen around the outside edge of the metal as shown, and then holding the edge tool firmly against the base so that the grindy bit is on the side of the ski, run it smoothly along the edge until the ink has just been removed. Concentrate. Don't place the wrong face of the tool on the base, and don't slip and gouge anything, or you'll wreck the ski. It's easy if you're careful and take it slowly.

If your edge tool comes with optional different grind angles, read the instructions and think carefully before deciding which to use.

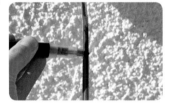

↑ **Mark the side of the rail with ink.**

↑ **Place the flat part of the tool firmly against the base of the ski.**

↑ **Press the abrasive file part hard against the side of the rail, and run it smoothly down the rail.**

↓ **The job isn't done until all the ink is gone.**

WAXING

Waxing your skis is actually very simple. You can use a special wax iron, available from larger ski shops, or you can use an ordinary domestic iron. Be warned though, once used for waxing, the iron will never be the same again. So use an old, retired iron. The steam feature is not required, so empty all the water out.

You will also need a scraper. You can buy a proper one, or just use a steel ruler or anything else that is stiff enough to scrape the wax off, straight, smooth and not sharp enough to damage the base. Plastic wax scrapers don't work well because they get destroyed by the metal edges of the skis.

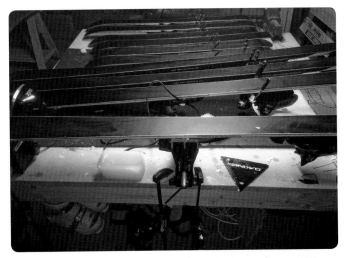

Skis should be at room temperature before waxing, so make sure you bring them indoors overnight before you begin. Heat up the iron to a medium heat, and dribble a small line of wax droplets along the base. Next, simply iron the wax all over the base. It doesn't need to be thick. Just make sure the whole area is wetted out with wax, right across from edge to edge. Leave the ski to cool back down to room temperature, and then scrape off all the wax as shown, using tip-to-tail strokes. This is physically quite strenuous, but otherwise the whole job is much easier than it sounds.

I like to use a wide metal scraper like the one shown so that there's no risk of gouging the base. However it is slightly bendy, which helps on skis that have a slight 'boat' shape or 'detune'.

That's it. Go skiing!

BASE GRIND

Once in a while, if there are very small scrapes or gouges in the base or rails, or after repairs to the sole of the ski, you will need to grind the base to remove dead material and make it smooth. Or, in fact, the right kind of unsmooth. You can do this at home with a belt sander, or a stone grinder. But there's a lot of stuff you need to know, and for the once in a blue moon this needs doing, it might be better value to take it to the shop and get a professional to do it.

⬅ **Drip the wax onto the base of the ski. You need less than you think.**

↙ **Iron the wax into the base in a circular motion so that the whole area is wet and shiny.**

⬇ **Scrape the wax off completely from tip to tail.**

The piste or trail map provided free of charge by most ski resorts can give you a pretty comprehensive guide to the routes, the lifts and the cafés, toilets and other amenities on the mountain. It's well worth getting hold of one for each member of your party. It's common these days for the resort to have a phone app or a downloadable map so that you can access the info on your phone, but as I've mentioned elsewhere, getting your phone out on the hill is fraught with hazard, and the battery won't last long in the cold. So I suggest a paper map. They make good souvenirs, too...

It's worth noting that these maps tend to be fairly schematic, and don't always make it entirely clear what is accessible from where. If you get lost, however, there should also be signposts similar to the one shown below, with the names and colours of the runs on them, and often other information to help you figure it out!

ACCESSING BACKCOUNTRY TERRAIN: When you pass beyond the ski area boundary, you are leaving the services including avalanche hazard reduction measures and trail grooming. You are entering a **HIGH RISK** are hazards including, but not limited to, avalanches, cliffs and hidden obstacles. You are at risk from these natura responsible for your decisions and actions, you may be responsible for the cost of your rescue and you waive a or property damage. Note: On each gate access, you must read the backcountry avalanche hazard forecast.

⬇ **You can expect to find cafés all over the mountain. And expect them to be expensive.**

⬇ **The base of the resort will have shops, cafés, and lifts as well as runs that feed into them.**

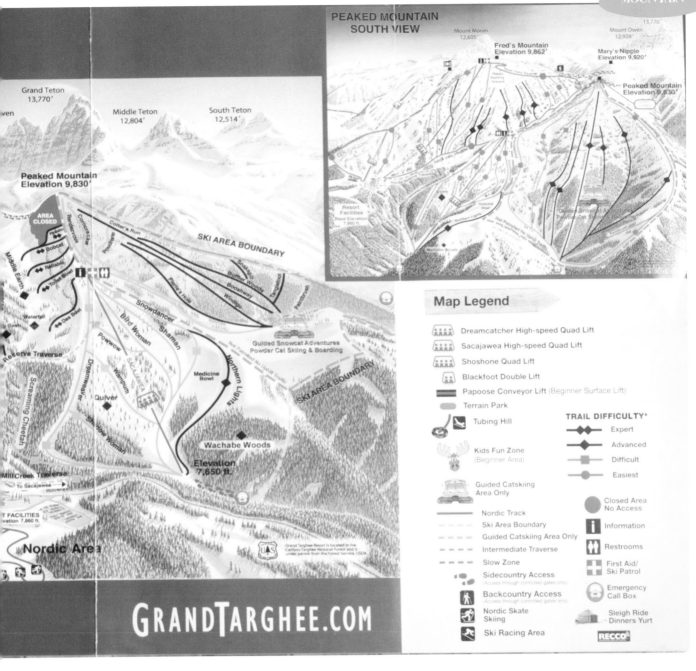

PEAKED MOUNTAIN
SOUTH VIEW

Mount Moran
12,605'

Fred's Mountain
Elevation 9,862'

Mary's Nipple
Elevation 9,920'

Mount Owen
12,928'

13,770'

Peaked Mountain
Elevation 9,830'

Resort
Facilities
Base Elevation
7,860 ft.

Guided Snowcat
Adventures Powder Cat Boarding

Grand Teton
13,770'

Middle Teton
12,804'

South Teton
12,514'

Peaked Mountain
Elevation 9,830'

AREA
CLOSED

SKI AREA BOUNDARY

Cotter's Run

Bobcat

Reliable

Toilet Bowl

Middle Earth

Das Boot

Waterfall

Reserve Traverse

Screaming Cheetah

Dreamweaver

Powwow

Shadow Woman

Snowdancer

Shaman

Bird Woman

Wampum

Quiver

SACAJAWEA

Medicine
Bowl

Northern Lights

Wachabe Woods

Elevation
7,650 ft.

Mill Creek Traverse

To Sacajawea

T FACILITIES
vation 7,860 ft.

Nordic Area

Guided Snowcat Adventures
Powder Cat Skiing & Boarding

SKI AREA BOUNDARY

Grand Targhee Resort is located in the
Caribou-Targhee National Forest and is
under permit from the Forest Service, USDA.

GRANDTARGHEE.COM

Map Legend

- Dreamcatcher High-speed Quad Lift
- Sacajawea High-speed Quad Lift
- Shoshone Quad Lift
- Blackfoot Double Lift
- Papoose Conveyor Lift (Beginner Surface Lift)
- Terrain Park
- Tubing Hill
- Kids Fun Zone (Beginner Area)
- Guided Catskiing Area Only

	TRAIL DIFFICULTY*
◆◆	Expert
◆	Advanced
■	Difficult
●	Easiest

- Nordic Track
- Ski Area Boundary
- Guided Catskiing Area Only
- Intermediate Traverse
- Slow Zone
- Sidecountry Access (Access through controlled gates only)
- Backcountry Access (Access through controlled gates only)
- Nordic Skate Skiing
- Ski Racing Area
- Closed Area No Access
- Information
- Restrooms
- First Aid/Ski Patrol
- Emergency Call Box
- Sleigh Ride Dinners Yurt

RECCO

⬇ **At the top of a lift, usually monitored by a lift attendant in a little hut.**

⬇ **Most resorts these days have a snow park, with ramps and other fun stuff to play on.**

I've lived on a ski hill for seven years now, and it's sometimes hard to remember what it was like being a holiday skier. I can remember the aches and pains of the unaccustomed exercise, but it was only when a friend, a very good skier and all-round intelligent guy, visited me the other day that I realised there's a lot that goes on in the resort that goes right over most people's heads. The nocturnal work of the piste-workers, for instance. The constant snowplough road clearing. The ceaseless efforts of the ski patrol. And how does all the food and beer get up the mountain?

You've probably heard the expression 'on the piste' and its opposite number, 'off-piste'. The word 'piste' is a French one, but well understood in most European resorts and sometimes heard in North America, too. It means track or trail. But therein lies the danger of translating words from one language to another. 'Ski run' might be a better translation.

When we say piste we generally* mean the groomed slopes that have been prepared for skiing on. These are prepared (usually overnight while skiers sleep or party) by caterpillar-tracked machines. Sno-Cat is a trademark, but a lot of people call them that. Otherwise, they might be called piste-machines, piste-bashers, (trail) groomers or just cats. As well as their tracked propulsion, which can take them up scarily steep icy slopes or powder, they usually

have a bulldozer-style scoop on the front and a comb-like trailer at the rear. With these two attachments, the machine can push the snow to where it's required, while literally combing the piste into the corduroy finish shown here that skiers know and love.

*Occasionally, a ski run will be called an ungroomed piste or trail. This makes the whole off/on-piste thing a bit more confusing than it needs to be, but luckily it is only very occasional. Additionally, the trails for cross-country skiing may also be called pistes in Europe, despite being flat.

We have to thank the mostly nocturnal work of the pisteurs for the quality of piste skiing in every resort!

In North America the piste is called a run, a trail, or sometimes, confusingly, a groomer. The expression 'off-piste' will be generally understood.

Off-piste describes everywhere that isn't on the piste. This could mean skiing off the side of the piste, or venturing further afield. Into the trees, perhaps, where the machines cannot go. Or hiking, driving or helicoptering into the inaccessible back-country, away from the resort, in search of un-tracked powder. This, too, is off-piste.

DIFFICULTY

For your guidance and safety, pistes are marked with an indication of their difficulty. The system is simple and good, for all that you'll hear people saying, usually in defence of their bruised egos, 'This run should never be a (insert classification here), what were they thinking?'

The system in North America uses signs with both colour and shape. Why, I couldn't say. These classifications are, however, quite consistent throughout the US, and Canada and Australia uses the same signage too. Elsewhere in the world, certainly Europe, Japan and New Zealand, systems of colours only are used.

EUROPEAN SYSTEM

There will usually be a baby slope (in the US this is called the bunny slope) that is barely sloping and suitable for first-time skiers. It doesn't tend to have a colour but there should be a sign, usually a patronising one implying that it would be embarrassing to be there if you're over four years old! You shouldn't have to brave a lift to use this slope, though it might have a conveyor belt or rope tow to help you back to the top.

Green – Very easy, suitable for beginners, never very steep.

Black – Advanced/expert skiers only. Consistently very steep, and usually with difficult terrain features including but not limited to moguls.

As well as signs to direct you to the correct piste, the sides of the trail are usually marked with poles which follow the same colour scheme.

In Japan, they use a similar system, but leave out the blue. Green is also used for beginner runs, red is for intermediate difficulty and black indicates expert terrain.

It's worth mentioning at this point that the gradient of a slope in Europe is usually measured in degrees, whereas in other countries it is often expressed as a percentaage. This can lead to all kinds of confusion, because they really are very different. See The Gradient Thing, page 86.

Blue – For confident beginners or intermediates. Should be able to snowplough turn both ways, preferably have a basic parallel turn, and stop on demand. Can be quite steep in places.

Red – For strong intermediates to advanced, who should be able to link quick parallel turns, and parallel stop. Can be very steep and/or feature moguls in places.

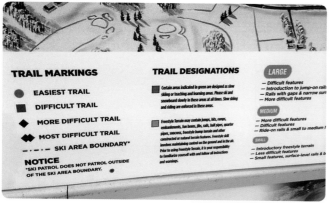

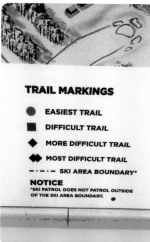

NORTH AMERICAN SYSTEM

Green circle with white centre – for first timers. This is usually the baby (or bunny) slope, not requiring the use of lifts.

Green circle – easy. Typically gradients of less than 25% (<15°).

Blue square – intermediate. Max gradients of 25–40% (15–22°)

Black diamond – advanced. Can be steeper than 40% (>22°)

Double black diamond – extreme. All kinds of terrain and madness.

In New Zealand, they leave out the red and add a 'double black'. So it's like the US system, without the shapes.

In most other countries, you might expect to find either the American or the European system. Chile, for instance, uses the European!

While the grading of each slope in a resort has been decided by people who know what they are doing, clearly it's not an exact science. One of the favourite topics of conversation amongst skiers is the relative difficulty of pistes with the same classification or the slopes in different resorts or countries. For instance, some skiers say that the green slopes in New Zealand are as difficult as some blue square runs in the US. It's important to realise that not only are the colours very approximate guidelines, but that other factors can make a big difference. How icy it is. Visibility. How heavily skied the slope has been. And perhaps most importantly, how tired you are or whether you had too much wine at lunchtime!

Equally, official wisdom recommends that you should have certain skills for certain slopes, but in reality you might be able to do a perfect parallel turn on a blue, and quite unable to pull it off on a steep icy red. So don't take it all too much to heart. Some people attach too much social status to being a 'black diamond' skier, or whatever. This leads to them blundering down a difficult slope in a quivering funk, and not looking half as cool as they would have done on something less steep. The sensible thing to do is work up from the bottom in each new resort you visit, and figure out at what level you have the most fun.

TERRAIN PARKS

In North America, an orange rectangle with rounded corners is often used to denote a 'terrain park' or other area containing man-made obstacles. In Europe there will usually be a written sign, and then the same colour scheme as for the pistes may be used to show how difficult each obstacle might be.

The park might contain any number of things to play with, but usually includes some freestyle jumps, metal rails to slide along, and perhaps a half pipe, all lovingly prepared with a combination of machinery and handheld shovels, sweat and tears. If you ever try to build a jump yourself, you'll see what an undertaking building these big ones must be! There is more about parks in the freestyle section (page 178).

As well as all the signage that informs us about the nature and difficulty of the various runs, there will be temporary signs put up by the ski patrol if a run has been closed for safety reasons, or to indicate an isolated hazard. One important one is a pair of crossed poles just uphill of an obstacle that should be given a wide berth. Another is the avalanche risk flags or signs, which are shown at every lift station, with different patterns or numbers for different degrees of snow instability.

A FEW EXAMPLES OF WARNING SIGNS

⬆ Artificial snow is a necessary evil but it can upset the unwary, hence this sign.

⬆ "Danger" doesn't necessarily mean imminent demise - in this case just that a slow moving button lift crosses a slow, green trail. But it could mean something more serious, so take note.

⬆ Perhaps the most important of all signs, and hence in several languages. Slow down!

⬆ This means "ungroomed (and very steep) run". Helpfully it's only in French!

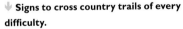
⬇ Signs to cross country trails of every difficulty.

⬇ A red cross with the telephone number, not of the Red Cross, but the local emergency number. Useful…

⬇ Skiers only. Not people on foot.

PHYSICAL PREPARATION

There are few sports in which physical preparation and training are as important. Skiing is not intrinsically dangerous, but many of us still harbour mental stereotypes of people coming home from a holiday with a limb in plaster. That shouldn't happen if you apply a bit of common sense on the mountain, but far more likely are aches, pains and fatigue that prevent you from enjoying the experience to the full.

Unfortunately, skiing is pretty difficult to simulate. For instance, when I first started cross-country skiing, I thought it would be a good idea to use one of those elliptical cross-trainer machines at the gym, but that didn't work. They may be useful for general cardio vascular training (we can have that argument another time), but they don't mimic the kinaesthetics of either classic or skate style closely enough to be much use. And it's harder still to mirror the motions and stresses of alpine skiing. A lot of skiing efforts are isometric, maintaining pressure without the muscles actually moving, and a whole lot more require a fairly big range of motion. Doing both at the same time requires that different types of muscle fibres are trained to fire at the same time. And that's difficult to do at home, or in the gym. But luckily not impossible!

WARMING UP (AND DOWN) AND STRETCHING

You're probably aware that it's a good idea to warm up and stretch before exercise, and to warm down and stretch again afterwards. This applies whether we're talking about skiing, or training for skiing. When it comes to the mountain, however, it's shocking how few people you see doing anything prior to getting on the lift. I expect they all warm up and stretch at home. Before travelling by car or bus to the hill, or walking, very slowly and carefully, in their ski boots, and then sitting motionless on a cold lift. All this as preparation for what is the

most violent and intensive workout that most amateurs, anyway, ever attempt. Doesn't seem too sensible to me!

If I've forgotten to do a warm-up, I usually take an easy couple of laps on a beginner (green) slope to get everything working as it should. Some skiers, however, intermediate and upwards, find this beneath their dignity. And anyway, it would still be better to prepare properly.

A young person might only need about ten minutes of gentle exercise to warm up, but for a middle-aged person, that's probably more like twenty minutes. So, walk to the hill/gym if you can, and then before you put on your skis, do some brisk uphill walking (almost jogging) on a treadmill, or on the snow. Swing your arms, jump up and down a bit. If this is all too much, maybe outdoor sport is not for you!

Once you are thoroughly warmed up, it's time to stretch. The photos show a set of stretches that you can do whether you are at the gym, or ready to ski. In all of these exercises, stretch slowly and hold the position for ten seconds. Don't bounce, and don't push it so far that it hurts.

⬆ **Place one foot at the other knee and stretch your arm to or past the toes of the straight leg.**

⬇ **Use this lift with the back straight. Push your hips up and hold the position. Repeat ten times.**

⬆ Push the small of your back against the ground, and pull alternate knees up close to your chest, slowly, and holding the stretch as shown. Ten times for each leg.

⬇ Turn one foot outwards as shown, and bend the upper body slowly as far as you can to that side. Alternate sides, ten each side.

⬆ Hold the bent leg as shown, and then stretch/rotate the upper body away from it. Hold, then switch and repeat with the other leg. Ten each side

⬇ *Slowly* pull your knees up towards your chest, and down again, ten times.

TRAINING

Let's turn our attention to basic fitness. Now, I'm sure some people are going to say you should have a full medical before taking up skiing, but let's be sensible. Skiing is strenuous, even when it's just downhill. But if you can walk up a flight of stairs, have no reason to believe you have a problem with altitude, and you have the mental strength not to commit yourself to slopes that are too much for you, I think you're going to be OK. Clearly, if you have some sort of pre-existing medical condition then you should consider the implications of that, or ask for professional advice. A medical professional, that is. I'm no use to you on that account.

You can train your body for skiing in preparation for a trip. You need to start a minimum of seven weeks before you plan to ski, and then I suggest you rest for a week before the trip. If you're really serious about your skiing, of course, you'll be training all year round (see Pursuit of Excellence, page 168)! You don't really need a gym membership to achieve this, although there are a lot of extra benefits to be gained, both practical and psychological, from going to a specific place of training, and having other people around you as you work out. If you actually go... if you're not going to stick to the plan, it would be much cheaper and less stressful to fail to work out at home.

Having said that the gym is better, there's nothing wrong with a home gym, and in fact most of these exercises can be done with household items and a pair of dumbbells, or even just heavy household objects like a sandbag or a fire extinguisher! How much weight you need to use for each exercise is best determined by a professional trainer, but the key is always to start small and work up slowly.

One of the main isometric exercises you'll use when skiing is quad and calf holding. This exercise isn't like anything you'd normally do, but luckily it's perfect training for downhill! Put your back against a smooth wall and sink down, shuffling your feet out, until you are in a sitting position as though on a dining chair. But without a chair. Hold the position for 20 seconds on day one, then increase it every three or four days.

⬇ **Another isometric exercise, this time for the core/abdominals. Beginners should hold it for 20 seconds, doing a little more each week.**

⬆ **Think it's all legs? Most skiers find their triceps, lats and shoulders are getting a workout too!**

⬆ **Power in the legs is of course all important.**

⬅ **This can also be done with a chair or coffee table and legs out in front of you.**

➡ **This rope work is a superb all-body exercise for skiing.**

After training or skiing, don't forget to cool down with gentle exercise for ten minutes, and then perform stretches again. This is key to preventing aches and injuries from surfacing overnight. Don't soak in a long, hot bath immediately after exercise – it feels great for your sore muscles, but this is a recipe for back problems, especially when your core is exhausted and not holding your posture quite as well as it should!

If you are only interested in some leisurely skiing, you still need to get fit for your visit to the slopes for a few months before you travel. No one, unless they ski day in and day out, is immune to the aches and pains from unaccustomed stress positions and muscle use that simply don't occur in (your) everyday life! And although a lot of books and fitness websites will tell you some basic moves you can try to remember to practise in the run up to a ski trip, it's difficult to push yourself as hard as gravity will on the mountain. But I would recommend trying to, because it's better all round to beast yourself a bit at home so that you don't waste half your holiday whinging in cafés.

CHAPTER TWO

BASIC STUFF

HEAD STUFF

I've banged on before about kinaesthetic awareness and the advantages of being a sensory learner, but I'm going to take it up a notch here. I'm no neuroscientist, but many of you will be familiar with the idea that there are two kinds of thinky bit in your brain. When I was a child these used to be called the conscious and the subconscious. Later on, brain research identified them as different areas of the brain, and inferred that we had a higher, more evolved bit calling the shots than some lesser species, like reptiles. Recent developments in brain scanning technology have continued to move the goal posts but none of this matters. As any sports scientist will tell you, thinking is rubbish.

Consider for a moment a game of chess. We (well, someone) can already make a supercomputer that will beat almost any living person at chess. Even the World Champions of chess with unpronounceable Russian names will be beaten occasionally by this miracle of modern technology. As long as you don't expect it to move the pieces. Because

in the real world of slightly random, even the best robot arm man has currently devised is about as dexterous at this job as a human toddler.

Thinking, as I said, is a bit pants compared to the incredibly complex task of moving stuff about. It's like learning to drive. When you first see the car veering a bit towards the kerb, and decide to turn the steering wheel in the opposite direction, you then have to wait the right amount of time and then turn it back again. Since you are reacting rather than anticipating, you're a bit late with both these actions. Having learnt a bit from that process, you don't make the mistake in such a big way every time, but it takes a while to iron out the problem. And until that time, you are weaving down the road like a great weaving thing.

Then, being only human, you have to go through the same experiential learning minefield each time you go out, although it will take you progressively less time to get in the zone.

KISS

So... it seems that the KISS principle continues to hold good (Keep It Simple, Stupid).

Eventually, after a great deal of driving or skiing experience, you will no longer have to remember to do things. This stage is reached when the practice has filtered down into a less thinky bit of the brain – the bit that even lizards have. How great would it be if there was a way to learn these incredibly complex kinetic processes without all this upfront thinking? Sadly, we can't. Although we can break the learning process into manageable chunks and then assemble them later. That's what any good teacher does. And we can also streamline the physical processes so that they are more learnable. Which is the exciting bit that I just learnt from a neuroscientist.

What makes moving stuff about so much more technical and difficult than thinking is the effect of 'noise'. I don't mean the distracting thunder of distant waterfalls or the crashing of waves. I mean noise in the control systems that we use to move our own body parts around, before we even wrap our oh-so-opposable thumbs around a pole or clip into our skis. When your brain sends a message to your hand, it gets messages back about what's happening, from the actual hand and also from the eyes. And this feedback tells the brain that it didn't all go quite as planned, partly because of noise inside the control system, and partly because of random effects outside of it, like unexpected forces affecting you. Wind, g-force and so on. On top of that, the message coming back to the brain about these deviations is a little bit wrong too, again because of noise. So the fact that the brain is able to tweak the action on the fly and make it all turn out reasonably well is frankly a bit of a miracle, but it does, because millions of years of evolution have gone into this.

Now, some people are just better at this than others, and I'm not talking about kinaesthetic awareness or different learning styles this time! It appears that the ability to hit a little white ball with a long stick so accurately that it goes into a hole 300 metres away, despite wind, rain and distraction, is in great part determined by the ability to manage noise in the brain, nervous system and musculature. A minimal amount of thinking goes into this, but most of it is under the radar – the autobiographical self comparing remembered past with anticipated future, and the motion bit comparing expected feedback with actual response and compensating accordingly.

Being a super-kinaesthete may well depend on things you no longer have any control over, like how you were carried when you were a baby or whether you ate all your Brussels sprouts. But there is something you can do now, and it's increasingly used by good coaches. Plan your movements to minimise negative consequences of noise. If you make a very complex motion to achieve a task, you are not only wasting a bit of energy, but you are exposing yourself to much more noise as you try to control the action. You can try this by putting your finger on something. If you go straight there with a simple single plane motion, like just bending your elbow, it's fairly accurate, but try to get there in a big complex arc and there will be a horrendous wobble near the end of the motion as you try to iron out the noise.

This is one of the reasons that some coaches and instructors still teach stem christies. Because if nothing else, they serve to illustrate an inefficient movement.

CORE STRENGTH

At various points in the book I mention core strength, core activation or core control. I think it's the most important physical element in all upstanding gravity sports. Your core muscles are the ones in the lower part of the torso, including but not limited to the 'six (or eight) pack' abdominals. All these muscles control your posture. If you break at the waist, bending forwards over your belt, these muscles will be part of the effort to recover, but it's a herculean task. Loss of posture, bending in the middle and the arm-waving and flailing that inevitably accompanies it, are the enemy. You must stay strong and taut in the middle, without being so rigid that the whole unit simply topples over!

SOFT LEGS

I also mention this a lot. One of the challenges of skiing, in common with most standing-on-stuff-type activities, is to keep the legs bent and relaxed while in a permanent state of readiness to straighten more to keep contact with the ground, or to bend more while resisting, damping out the bumps. It's really hard to explain, but if you spend more time in a sort of alert crouch, you will come to understand it.

⬇ **Strong core, soft legs, safe arms...**

SKIING MECHANICS AND MOTION

We've done the science bit, as it applies to all skis. Now we have to consider some other factors. To do that, we need to wind the clock back to the earliest days of skiing, when skis where straight planks of wood.

In order to turn a simple ski, it was necessary to lift it up and move it to point in the direction the skier wanted to go. This is still done today in certain circumstances, such as on cross-country skis, or in difficult terrain, and it's called a step turn.

It's not hard to discover, though (and I'm sure our ancestors did), that tilting the ski a bit lets you push it across the snow without lifting it. This feels a lot more stable and secure, because you stay on two legs, and forms the basis of the snowplough (wedge) turn, the stem turn, and eventually leads to the parallel turn, where the skis begin to bend and to carve more efficiently through the turn without skidding. However, as discussed in the history section (see page 12), at some point in the 1800s, skiers started to discover that better ski design could help them to make better turns. And that's where this part of the story begins.

When the skiers of Telemark and neighbouring Christiania developed better skis, the two main features that they introduced were camber and sidecut. The natural weight distribution on a plank is such that the foot area sinks into the snow, and less weight is applied to the ends of the ski. The ski will glide better and hold its edge better if the weight can be distributed further, and that's what camber achieves. Sidecut means that when the ski is tilted over in the snow (called edging), the ski will be forced to bend and this will facilitate a carving turn. The more sidecut, the tighter the radius and more dramatic the turn.

Modern skis for off-piste skiing are sometimes bent the other way over some or all of their length. That's called 'rocker'. It's a recent development, but now the rocker/camber shapes of skis are getting increasingly complex and varied, depending on the purpose of the ski.

Older skis had moderate amounts of camber and sidecut because too much of either would clearly cause problems with certain actions. Sidecut improves turns but harms speed and straight-line stability. Camber, too, improves speed and edge grip only up to a point. The old-style skiers used one set of skis for everything, so these developments weren't taken to extremes.

With a limited amount of sidecut and simple camber, it was necessary to learn some skilful body language in order to force the ski to bend and carve a powerful turn, and despite the developments in modern equipment that have made these skills less necessary, they are still useful in order to get the very best out of your skis even today.

That's why you'll see some distinctive body language from many an experienced skier, with a rising and falling motion that weights and un-weights the skis. This not only allows the skis to change edges easily but powers them up to bend them and drive them into the snow during the turns. The timing of this is absolutely critical, and is best learned by following your ski instructor and mimicking his movements (see page 44).

Mow to carry your skis, put them on, take them off. Stuff like that.

Modern skis and boots seem somewhat over-technical. They have to be clunky, chunky mechanical devices because the forces that act on them are frankly enormous, even for a recreational skier. You don't want your feet twisting around in your boots, or your bindings breaking, or your skis snapping. The only light bit of the whole combo is the poles, because they are sort of surplus to requirements. Icing on the cake, so to speak. If you sit on them they might bend or break, but you can usually get home without them!

PUTTING ON YOUR SKI BOOTS

If your ski boots are correctly fitted, as they should be, it'll be easy to slide your feet into them. Usually the boot has a soft liner – make sure that your foot is snug inside, and that the tongue of the liner is settled into the right place, before you try to tighten the boots. The one thing you can't have is any kind of folds or lumps in the liner or your socks. Make sure too that where your thermals end and socks begin, there isn't any kind of ridge or seam that's going to be inside the boots. Anything like this will cause pressure or friction, and very possibly blisters and pain!

Once the liner's settled, do up the boots one cam clip at a time, and make sure it isn't tight on one spot and loose in another. The final adjustment is the power strap, which is essential for transmitting leg movement to the ski.

Some people find it easy to walk in ski boots. Most don't. It depends on your physiology, your fitness and flexibility, and a little bit your attitude! If your boots have a walk switch to release the ankle for walking, use this, but don't forget to lock it before skiing! If not, you might find that undoing the boots for walking is comfortable for you. Or you might not, and just have to suck it up.

⬇ **Cam buckle (L) and walk switch (R).**

CARRYING YOUR SKIS

Skis can be clipped together using their brake levers as shown. This makes them easier to stack or carry. The two main ways to carry skis are on the shoulder, or using the poles.

Cross-country or telemark skis don't have

↗ **Using the leashes of tele skis to hold them together.**

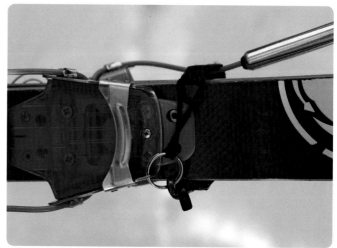

⬇ **If not, this is a good reason to use the pole carry method!**

⬇ **In deeper snow the poles are useful for clearing the boots first.**

brakes. There may be another good way to attach them. Sometimes they have leashes or velcro straps supplied.

If you're holding the skis directly, you're going to want your ski gloves on, because the metal edges are cold and sharp. These same edges will trash your gloves unless they are reinforced. This is one advantage of the pole carry. The disadvantage of the pole carry is that the edges eventually (long term) damage the wrist straps of the poles and you have to be a bit careful with front-to-back balance, as the skis can also slide out of the loops.

Another option is to use a backpack that has straps for equipment on the outside. This is the usual choice of the backcountry skier who will be hiking off and on, and has avalanche equipment to carry inside the pack, but it's also very useful for the resort skier. A small pack is great for carrying extra insulation, water, lunch, spare socks in case they get wet, and on the way home you will be the envy of your tired

friends. The down side is that if you're the only person wearing one, you become the pack horse for everyone else's spare stuff.

CLIPPING IN

On arrival at the lifts or slope, you need to put on your skis. There should be somewhere flat to do this, but if not, rule number one is to place your skis across the slope so that they don't try to slide away once you're in. Generally there's no left and right ski.

It's a good idea to stick the poles in the snow either side of the skis for support as you clip in, but first make sure there are no big lumps of snow or ice adhering to boots or bindings – the poles are handy for clearing that away, or you can rub the snow off the boots on the toe piece of the binding as shown.

⬇ **For longer distances, or added convenience, there are a few ways to hike with skis that keep your hands free. One is to buy a special harness for your skis and poles.**

⬆➡ **The front of the boot has a sort of protruding bit at the toe.**

⬆ **Push the toe of the boot into the front part of the binding as shown, make sure your foot is aligned straight along the ski, and then press the heel down hard until it clicks firmly into place. Lift and twist to make sure it's locked in. Then do the other foot. You can tell the boots are locked in properly when there's a solid clunk and the brake levers flip up as shown.**

Alpine ski bindings are released in an accident by pulling or twisting force, but this can't easily be done deliberately. The way to remove the skis is to press down on the lever at the heel part of the binding by hand, with a pole or with the other ski/boot. Skiers become quite slick at this very quickly.

⬇ **Telemark skis are donned in a similar way to alpine ones, but after sliding the nose piece of the boot into place (it's typically longer than on an alpine boot), the springloaded rear part of the binding is clipped into place by hand. The bindings are released in the same way. Note leash**

→ **Cross-country skis feature a number of different binding systems, but all work on roughly the same principle – a bar under the toe clips into the binding either by downward foot pressure, or by hand. The bindings are released by pushing on the front of the clip by hand or with a ski pole.**

HOLDING THE POLES

The handle part of the ski pole often has a moulded finger grip shape, which goes at the front. This matters because some poles are curved or kinked. There may also be a left and right pole for the same reason. Attached to the handle, you'll usually find a webbing strap, which may or may not be adjustable. Most people just put their hand through the strap as shown.

→ **Pass your hand through the strap and grip the handle of the pole. Adjust the strap if necessary.**

↑↓ **There are other types of pole retention. This race combo has a special clip on the handle that matches to an integral loop in the glove.**

→ **Some skiers contend that the correct method for downhill skiing is to pass the hand up through the loop as shown and then grip the strap against the handle. It feels a little weird but allows you to release the pole more easily if you need to use your hand, and reduces the likelihood of the strap coming off your wrist in a fall.**

When actually skiing, try to keep your hands in front of your body and the arms bent into an 'O' shape as shown.

POSTURE

Once you've got your skis on, stand up nice and straight but without locking your knees. Make sure that you are symmetrical and upright and in particular that your spine is in a good but relaxed posture. Bend your elbows as shown so that the sticks are upright and the forearms are horizontal. DO NOT break at the waist if you feel wobbly! This causes all kinds of problems. The right thing to do is bend your knees and sink closer and closer to the ground if you're afraid of falling.

MORE POSTURE

One thing that's quite important when wearing two planks is how our bodies present our feet to the ground. You may have addressed this at the boot buying/hiring stage but if not, it's a good idea to look at it now.

Most people's feet are prone to tilt inwards or outwards when standing, and this can be caused by a number of things. Boot fitting can take account of any slight pronation (tilt inwards) or supination (tilt outwards) with the use of shims under the feet, or adjustment on the boot itself. In some cases an adjustment can be made to how the boot addresses the binding or the binding can be tilted on the ski. It's essential for high-performance skiing later on. But the biggest cause of skis not sitting flat on the snow comes from the legs. Pulling the knees together into a slightly 'knock-kneed' posture will dig the inner edges of the skis into the snow. A bow-legged posture will dig in the outside edges. So, once standing on skis, you can test yourself a little with the following exercise, which very quickly teaches your legs to keep the skis flat or at least to feel the fine edge control required not to trip over.

Standing normally, slide the skis apart keeping them parallel at all times, and then squeeze them back together. Repeat until you've forgotten to think about it! If it's hard to move them apart, you are over-supinating. If it's more difficult to pull them back together, you're over-pronating. Of course, it's possible to do both. But do the exercise a few times and your body will sort it all out.

ANKLE FLEX EXERCISE

It seems expedient to mention now, that most skiing activities are done leaning slightly forwards. There will be more about this in other parts of the book, but for now I just want to mention another exercise, one that makes sense to have in your toolbox before you go to work

on any other techniques. The soles of your boots are for all intents and purposes bolted down flat and completely stiff. When you're standing up straight, your weight is acting straight down onto your heels. As you bend the knees and sink down a little, your ankles should flex forwards and you will feel the pressure of your shins against the front of the boot. Sink down some more, and although your centre of gravity doesn't move forwards much, this pressing forwards you can feel in the boot is actually transferring the pressure forward towards the centre of the ski. It is important just to sink down vertically to achieve this. If you bend at the knees and waist as you would to sit down, you are not flexing the ankle to press the boot forward, and the back of the skis will be too weighted and resist your efforts to turn them.

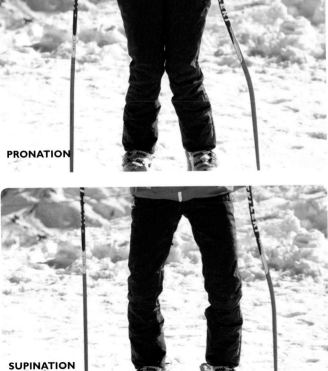

PRONATION

SUPINATION

ANKLE FLEX

GETTING AROUND

The first thing many people attempt is going downhill. That's not so clever. First of all, if you're a beginner or just haven't skied for a long time, it's best to practise getting around on the flat, and moving up and down very gentle slopes without sliding downhill. Work with gradients that are within your current ability. At the beginning, that's going to be no gradient at all. Let's start somewhere flat!

A good exercise for beginners is to practise walking and scooting wearing only one ski. This way the skis can't get crossed over or otherwise tangled up, and there will always be one boot firmly planted to stop you from sliding off out of control. Once you are confident scooting along and turning around, wearing two skis will be a bit less daunting.

Next, we should figure out how to get around on the flat with both skis on, using a combination of stepping and poling. It's not difficult to see that you can lean forward and sort of push yourself along with your poles. This is the first thing that comes to most people's minds, but it's not a very good way to get around. You're trying to move your whole weight with some of the smallest muscles in your arms. A better strategy is to tilt the poles back and slide the skis forward one at a time, or even to lift them and step a little. You can often see kids just walking with their little skis on, even without the use of poles. With poles, you can step one ski forward and then give a little push to glide it, and the repeat for the other ski. Using the poles to stop yourself slipping back as you walk is much better than trying to use them to propel yourself.

⬆ One way to turn around is to lift and step each ski a few degrees at a time. There are better ways, but for now this will do the trick.

⬇ You can walk the skis along on the flat, assisted by your poles if needed. This helps to remind you that you can lift the skis and move them independently.

THE FALL LINE

The brains of people who have grown up in the mountains have a different bit of wiring from those of the recreational visitor. They have an instinctive grasp of what is known as 'the fall line'. The fall line is absolutely fundamental to our understanding of gravity sports, but luckily the local advantage need not prevail. It's a very simple concept. You just have to remember to think about it!

Imagine that you placed a round ball, like a soccer ball, on the hillside and let it go. It would roll downhill. That's not rocket science. The fall line is the line on the ground it would follow. Still not blowing your mind, huh? So how does it come about that most people don't 'see' the fall line? I think it comes from our education. Most people, when asked to point out which way is downhill, are either misled by scale, 'downhill is in the direction of the bottom of the mountain', and by route 'downhill is in the direction along this road that leads to the bottom of the hill'.

Understandable mistakes. But when skiing we are only interested in the tilt of the actual bit under our feet. And this can be sloping from left or right, or uphill, while we are still looking directly at the bottom of the hill. All you have to do is to look at your boots, and the ground for a metre (3ft) or so all around, and think 'which way would a ball roll from where my feet are now?' That is the fall line.

If you do need to go uphill, make sure that your skis are at 90° across the fall line. Take your time to be sure of this if you don't know how to deal with being wrong about it! Keep the ski bases horizontal so that the uphill edge digs into the slope, and step up with the uphill ski first. Bring the lower ski up to join it, and repeat. It's slow going but you can ascend any slope this way.

At first, practise going up a hill that has a wide, flat run-out at the bottom of it. Most nursery slopes (bunny slopes) are designed like that. This means that if you end up descending out of control because you can't do anything yet, it won't (shouldn't) end badly.

⬆️⬇️↘️ **The fall line is indicated by the arrow. Keep your skis at 90° across the fall line and you can step uphill one ski at a time.**

The next level after walking and sliding the skis is to think about skating them. If you already know how to skate, on ice, or roller skates/blades, this will come easily to you. The skis are longer though, so you must focus on the tails and not treading on them. The principle is simple enough – lift and twist one ski to point away to the side and lunge in that direction pushing with the side of the other ski. Let ski 1 glide as far as it wants to and then repeat on the other side. It will take a while to find the right angles for your skis and this varies depending whether you are going up or down or along the flat, but practice makes perfect. Once it all feels natural, you can add some extra power by pushing with the poles. See cross-country skiing, page 126 for more detail on ways to skate efficiently.

Skating sometimes leaves a trail of V-shaped impressions in the snow that look like the skeleton of a fish, particularly when skating/walking up a steep slope. For this reason, uphill skating technique is sometimes called 'herringbone'.

← **Push with the left leg, push with the right, use the poles when you can.**

→ **Lean into the skating ski and fully extend the pushing leg.**

↓ **When you are confident you can make bigger steps and skating moves.**

↘ **You can use a combination of skating and stepping. Don't be afraid to lift your skis and move them around!**

BEGINNER TECHNIQUE – THE SNOWPLOUGH

The snowplough technique is the way to turn your skis and to stop once you are sliding down the hill. It's pretty essential – you'll see even the most expert skiers use it now and again. When you are first starting out, the snowplough is everything.

Small children find it very easy to snowplough. That's because they are made of rubber and magic. Actually for an adult, it requires quite a bit of flexibility and muscle control, which is why you should be reasonably fit and have warmed up and stretched before skiing, as described on page 54.

The technique is to brush the tails of the skis apart, while keeping the tips of the skis close, maybe a handspan apart. This can be easy or difficult depending on the surface and whether you tend to pronate or supinate. But either way, it's going to call into play a whole bunch of muscles that you don't use in everyday life. The trick is to use your thigh muscles to spread your legs, and your feet to turn the toes inwards at the same time. The skis will naturally roll onto their inside edges.

Try to adopt the position while you are on the flat. To return to a normal parallel skiing position, it's often easier to lift up one ski and bring it next to the other, because otherwise the skis' inside edges

drag against the snow. Next, try it while heading down a (very) gentle slope. Remember to use all the muscles you can find to resist the skis getting out of position. The wedge shape will slow you down, and the more spread the wedge or the greater pressure on the inside edges, the more braking you will get. Just ease off the muscular tension to go faster, or crank it on to hit the brakes. It's a lot easier than it looks, as long as the slope is gentle. Concentrate on two things – keeping your knees a little bit flexed, and stopping the skis from following their natural direction and crossing over each other!

In the US, the snowplough is sometimes called 'pizza' and the parallel position 'french fries'. It took me a while to work out what they were saying. Years, in fact!

Now that you've got the braking thing down, the next stage is to steer your snowplough, wedge or pizza. This is even easier! Shift your weight (just a little) towards one ski, and the wedge will start to turn in the direction that ski is pointing. It's a bit of a surprise to

⬇ **Keep the knees bent a little. Once you are confident you can step or jump your feet into this position, but for now keep both feet planted in the snow.**

↑ **It is astonishing what a tight turn you can make with a snowplough technique, even going at a snail's pace!**

those of us used to steering bicycles, or skateboards, by leaning to the inside of the turn, but it makes sense if you just remember that you'll go the way the more emphasised ski is pointing. Do it carefully at first, and remember to shift your weight over whichever foot. If you try to lean, you may topple. If you try to push against the ski by straightening your leg, you will get in a similar muddle. So just get into your snowplough position, and then shift your hips towards one foot or the other.

Modern hyperbolic skis will try to turn towards each other once on their inside edges. While this makes it easier to get into the position while skiing forwards, it also means you have to use a bit of muscle to hold the skis in place. Small children sometimes get around this problem by maxing out into a Y-shape so that they don't have to use any force, but they only get away with it, as I said before, because they are made of rubber. Adults need the suspension of bent knees, and not to be at the limits of motion!

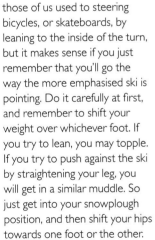

↑ **The hardest part of the reverse wedge is not to cross the tails of the skis.**

← **Look over your shoulder while reversing!**

REVERSE WEDGE

It's perfectly possible to snowplough while going backwards, and it might be as well to have a little go at it before getting too enthusiastic on the hill. It's all too easy to start pointing uphill and realise you have nothing in your toolbox to deal with that. The truly skilful can ski backwards and steer using a reverse wedge, but just being comfortable with adopting the position to avoid sliding away downhill is good enough for most people.

USING THE SNOWPLOUGH

Going down the hill with the brakes on is pretty tiring. And dull. That's the reason that good skiers descend in a series of Ss. So the next thing to do is to practise turning one way and then the other, wending your continuous wiggly way down the hill, controlling your speed as you do.

When descending the hill with a continuous snowplough starts to wear a bit thin, it's time to think about skiing parallel. Adopt a snowplough position. Brake until you are confident to turn. Turn until your downhill ski is pointing the way you want to go. Bring the uphill ski quickly into line. Ski parallel.

THE STEM TURN

Back in the dawn of time (the 1920s anyway) any turn using the wedge techniques was called a 'stem turn'. Stemming is the old word for wedging, it seems. A turn that skidded the skis around without using the telemark stance was called a 'christie' – because of the theory that this technique comes from the town of Christiania (the old name for Oslo) as opposed to Telemark. The early 20th-century pioneers of giving names to everything called the transitional wedge to parallel turn a 'stem christie'.

One final word of warning before we move on. When you sweep or step the backs of your skis out to form a wedge, be mindful of those next to you, since parking your skis on top of theirs may lead to upset. Equally, don't stand or ski too close to people, especially beginners, who might want to snowplough.

DROPPING IN

You can stand with your skis across the fall line, surveying the valley below, looking for all the world like a real pro. But how do you drop into the fall line and ski away? Let me count the ways...

Your uphill edges are digging into the snow, stopping you from slipping. If you stop digging them in, by relaxing your stance and moving your body, particularly your hips, down the fall line, the skis will start to slip. Keeping your weight pressed forward in the boots will bias this slippage towards the front of the skis turning downhill.

Skiers who are on a slope that is challenging for their skill/ strength/nerve sometimes like to use the poles for support on the downhill side, and to make the turn around them. This extra point of contact with the snow can also help with the body language to get the drop-in started.

There are several modes you can use to make the turn. Let's look first at the snowplough (below). If you brush the uphill ski out to form the wedge, you're already halfway there! Just shunt your weight forward and pressure the outside ski all the way through the turn. This has the advantage that you are controlling your speed with the wedge throughout.

If you are a confident parallel skier, wanting to drop in and pick up speed, you might want to do it another way. The skier above has done almost the opposite, sweeping the downhill ski to point down the slope with the other one coming into line almost immediately (that could be with braquage or by means of a step), again using the poles as a confidence assist.

The super-confident skier will not need to pivot around the poles, but will simply initiate the turn from a standstill just as if it had been from a traverse or carving (below).

Another way to turn the skis into the fall line is to jump and rotate through 90°. You can practise the jumping on the flat at first, and then take it to the hill. It's easiest if you rotate your upper body first, jump second, and then rotate the legs into line third. If you jump, you will want to land exactly in the fall line, or if you don't, with a very good understanding of the fall line so that you can respond quickly to the transverse forces with the appropriate amount of edge.

FALLING DOWN AND GETTING UP

'Fall down seven times – get up eight.'
Japanese proverb

If you progress methodically and carefully through the process of learning to ski, there is little reason to fall down. But it's in our nature to push the boundaries of human endeavour a little, or a lot, so everyone falls sooner or later.

I can't stress enough that I think the biggest mistake people make while skiing is to take on slopes that are just too steep for them. Having said that, I have to add that looking back at my experience in professional sport, the biggest thing that held me back was my unwillingness to fail or fall down, even in practice, mostly because of a feeling that I would look bad to my peers if I did so.

Think of it thus: in sport, as in life, it's not a straight line from starting out to success. It's a very wiggly one, in fact, and there are few short cuts. There are many components in the formula for achieving your goals, but not one of them works quite as well as simple perseverance. If you do not stay the distance, you do not reach the destination.

It behoves us all to decide how ambitious we are, and what we want to achieve with our skiing. And no matter how lofty our ambitions, we should not take unnecessary risks. But if you can fall down safely, fall down. The more you get up, the less you will be afraid of falling.

Falling in soft snow is like falling into one of those foam pits that children (and really extreme athletes) play in. It's almost less stressful than being upright. Falling onto hard packed snow or even ice is a different matter, and can be a bit of a nasty bump.

Many people advise you to relax your body in the event of a fall. Other useful tips include 'Don't put your arms out to stop yourself!' Well, that's all very well, but you can't reprogram yourself this easily, so I guarantee in an unexpected fall you will a) tense up, and b) put your arms out. So here's some advice to ameliorate the inevitable, instead of some pointless stuff you can't do.

As a beginner, most of your falls will be on almost flat ground. If you know/fear the fall is coming, the trick is to be nearer to the ground. Bend everything, and sink down low. That way, you won't have so far to fall, and if it's a 'high side' type incident, you won't whack into the ground with a lot of leverage, but instead 'roll with it'. There's only one thing to remember – bend everything, get down low.

Some people instinctively get their heads low by bending at the waist, but forget to bend everything else. The important thing is actually to get your bottom down low.

If you sink down and sit on the back of your skis, you can set off an 'accelerating out of control' scenario. So as your posterior altitude tends to zero, think about throwing yourself one way or the other, to avoid this and so that your bottom doesn't land on the skis. If there's a

If you have no skis on, recover them and place them across the fall line. Stand below them. Then put on the downhill ski as shown. This way, the ski can't slide away because your boot is in the way. Once that ski is on, and its edge firmly embedded in the snow, you can step up the other boot to the uphill ski. Use poles to stabilise you during this operation. It is a bit wobbly!

choice between falling uphill or downhill, uphill is infinitely preferable. If you have the recommended pole grip, with your arms O-shape and hands close in front, this will help you fall safely and tidily as well.

That's all I have to say about falling on gentle slopes. On a steep slope it's a bit different. If you are moving slowly and things go wrong, by all means employ the same strategy and sink gracefully to the ground, binning it on the uphill side at the last moment. But more likely you'll be going fast, and have time to make a short exclamation like 'Whaa' before you hit the ground in a random posture. The good news here is that falling on the steeper ground never hurts as much as it looks as if it should. Instead of stopping suddenly, you will slide for some distance before coming to rest. Let the slide slow down naturally, trying to keep skis and poles lifted out of the snow, unless you are going to hit something. If possible, slide feet first so that if you do hit any obstacle, it's with your boots not your head.

Once you have stopped, you will ideally have your feet on the downhill side. If not, twizzle round on your bottom until that is the case. Then, bend your knees to get your backside as close to your feet as you can, and get up facing across the fall line. If you are still wearing your skis, you're back in business. If not, employ the following strategy for putting them on!

TO POLE OR NOT TO POLE?

A lot of people will tell you that the correct way to get up is using the poles, but as a beginner, you may well practise without poles. It's important to be able to get up without them. Also, trying to heave on the poles can put your shoulders in an unstable position. Finally, in soft snow it doesn't work. This getting-up sequence shows how to push yourself up with your hands even without letting go of the poles.

➡ **Once you have got the skis across the fall line and your bottom close to your boots, it should be easy to get up. Just make sure you don't lift the skis out of the snow in case they slide away from you!**

⬆ **You know how to snowplough. So you can always stop this way. It can be quite a strain if it's too steep, though.**

⬆ **Keeping the skis horizontal and across the fall line, you can stand around indefinitely with zero effort.**

S o, you can make your way around on a slope, point yourself downhill and hooray! You're skiing! But you need to be able to stop.

Your first attempts at stopping will have involved increasing the

amount of spread or edge you applied to your snowplough stance, crashing into something soft, or else throwing yourself to the ground like a four-year-old having a tantrum. It's time to do it with a little more style and grace. The first port of call is still the snowplough or wedge, but if space allows, it's easier and more elegant to turn across the slope to stop.

The J turn is the name skiers sometimes use for turning until almost skiing uphill. This will, inevitably, cause you to stop, and it's worth practising that a few times on a gentle slope. You don't really need to ski uphill, however. Just turn smoothly, increasing the pressure on the wedge and in particular the downhill ski, until said downhill ski is pointing directly across the fall line as you come to rest. Step the other ski into a parallel shape, and commence standing around looking professional! This exercise not only enables you to stop gracefully, but leads directly into the next phase of learning turns, and ultimately parallel skiing.

The next exercise familiarises the skier with balance and being aware of the amount of weight on each ski. Lift one ski just a little, keeping it level, and concentrating on keeping the other leg bent. Then

↑ **Lifting one ski and then the other.**

↑ **This little jump builds up a lot of confidence.**

↑ **Bend down and touch the outside of your boots with your hands.**

put it down and lift the other. Try it stationary at first, and then while moving down the slope.

People's ability to balance on one leg varies, and in particular it deteriorates as we get older. But if you are feeling very good about the exercise above, consider trying to hop on one leg while the other ski is raised. If you can do that without mishap, try to hop and turn, so that you spin around on the spot over the course of a number of hops. Not while you are moving. That would be silly.

Another very good confidence builder is to jump on the flat. Bend your knees and spring, concentrating on keeping the skis level and the regulation distance apart. Remember to bend your knees again as you descend, to absorb the impact. Once you are doing it all right, try it while skiing slowly downhill, and then while skiing faster!

The 'boot touch' exercise is good for joining up the dots in your kinaesthetic feedback loop (see Head Stuff page 60) and for getting used to moving your body up and down while skiing. Try it while stationary, and then later while skiing do several reps at a time on the way down the piste.

The final exercise in this section is what I call the 'Need For Speed'. While I will keep reiterating that you should stick to slopes that are not too steep for you, there's also a tendency for many skiers to spend their whole time braking and scrubbing at the snow with their edges. This is a lot of effort and noise and wear and tear when there's often just no need. Sometimes it's good just to let the skis run free, and this exercise will help you to feel OK about that. So, after picking somewhere safe, drop in to the fall line and just stay there, skis parallel and flat and pointed straight down. Adopt a racing crouch if you want! Count to one, two, three, and then stand up and make a J-turn-type stop. When your heart rate is back within an acceptable range, go again. Try to build up the count until you can reach ten. It might be expedient to insert some elephants (one elephant, two elephants, three...) in order to stop yourself simply counting faster!

→ **Count to ten. Or whatever seems appropriate.**

VISIBILITY

In a perfect world, we'd all go skiing on perfect fresh snow that only fell at night, and every day would be a bluebird day without a cloud in the sky.

Sadly, that's not real life at all. Sometimes it snows for days on end. Sometimes it rains, even in the mountains in winter. And sometimes it's cloudy. Mountains, being the tall things that they are, follow a different set of rules from more low-lying geography. Sometimes you can escape into the sunshine above the clouds. But sometimes, you're just in them.

If you are lucky enough to be able to choose your skiing days after paying close attention to weather forecasts and the like, then you may be able to make the best use of any clear days on the hill. Even

then, however, you may get it wrong and find yourself in poor visibility. Those of us who go away on a ski trip for a week or more, perhaps booked months in advance, are at the mercy of the weather. So, what to do on the less than perfect days?

In most activities where it matters, like scuba diving, or driving, visibility is measured in distance. As this distance reduces, the fun level goes down and the stress level goes up, until you rather wish you'd stayed at home. But in skiing terms, there are basically two types of visibility. One is the usual 'being able to see stuff' kind, which can be measured in distance. As the 'vis' deteriorates, you first cease to enjoy the view, but can still see people and signposts and things. Once the visibility is down to ten metres or so (30ft), you can no longer ski faster than a walking pace, or have any idea where you're going. And that's no fun. All you can do is find your way down, or to a bar, by following the line of coloured poles at the side of the piste. In really bad vis, you can see yourself and your skis, and pretty much nothing else. At this point it isn't even safe to move, because your sense of which way is up and down relies more on your eyesight than you would believe!

The other sort of bad vis

doesn't stop you seeing people and things, but deprives you of the ability to see the snow properly. This is often called 'flat light'. It happens when then light from the sun is so diffused by the clouds or reflection from the snow that there are no shadows. Shadows are the only way we have of seeing the shape of clean, white snow. Without them, it's impossible to read the terrain, and even on a fairly smooth and easy piste, you can find yourself falling over and/or losing control and crashing into things, even though you can see them perfectly well! There are different sorts of flat light, from grey and dull to really bright, and to add to the complications, generally the light is flat when the vis distance is short, too.

The general solution to the former problem is to stop skiing. Just get off the mountain, or at least stop and rest up until you can see well enough for it to be safe and fun. The flat-light problem, on the other hand, can be improved by switching to suitable lenses for the conditions. See page 41 for the different lens choices a skier might consider.

TREES

If, however, the location and your skill level allows it, it can be worth looking into the trees. Sometimes, just being able to see something, anything, is all we need in order to orientate ourselves, and being surrounded by trees can be the answer. Even a line of trees near the piste can help the skier to focus. Off-piste, wooded areas also have some other magical properties – in flat light the perspective the trees give can help with reading the snow underfoot, and if the problem is that it is actually snowing, for some reason this seems to be less of a problem in the woods. Before you dive off-piste into the forest, however, you must be a very good skier. Check out the tree-skiing section on page 155.

NIGHT SKIING

Many resorts offer the opportunity to go skiing at night, on pistes that are illuminated by floodlights. This sounds like a recipe for disaster, but in fact the visibility while night skiing is very good. Because the lights are relatively low down (usually they're on top of the lift pylons), there are very clear shadows on the snow and if anything it makes the terrain easier to see and interpret than in broad daylight! It is quite important to take fairly light-coloured goggles, though. The dark grey or polarising kind won't be great in this low light level. Rose, orange or yellow lenses work just fine.

⬆ **Go back to a slope where you are actually poling and skating to try to increase the speed as you drop in at the top, and practise skilful skiing. It's more fun.**

⬇ **Angle (in degrees) and gradient (or grade) in per cent are very different. Here's a graph.**

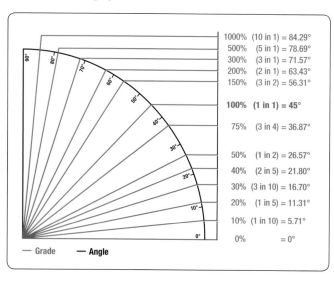

1000%	(10 in 1)	= 84.29°
500%	(5 in 1)	= 78.69°
300%	(3 in 1)	= 71.57°
200%	(2 in 1)	= 63.43°
150%	(3 in 2)	= 56.31°
100%	**(1 in 1)**	**= 45°**
75%	(3 in 4)	= 36.87°
50%	(1 in 2)	= 26.57°
40%	(2 in 5)	= 21.80°
30%	(3 in 10)	= 16.70°
20%	(1 in 5)	= 11.31°
10%	(1 in 10)	= 5.71°
0%		= 0°

— Grade   — Angle

I can't emphasise strongly enough this one fact. It's the most important thing in the whole book. Always be conservative about the steepness of slopes you undertake.

The number one cause of the following ski problems:
■ Not having a fun time
■ Practising and reinforcing terrible technique
■ Suffering personal injury or indignity
■ Falling out with your partner or other friends

Is 'being on a slope that's too steep for you'!!! OK, I admit some après-ski-related activities do give steepness a run for its money, but you get my point, I'm sure.

Most of the time, the steepness and difficulty of any run will be indicated by its classification on the maps or signage. Sometimes this actually does tell you how steep it is, but usually the width and nature of the slope has been taken into account as well. So whether a run is a green or a black tells you something, but not everything, about the gradient.

If you can find out what the actual gradient is like, before committing to a run, please do. But the info is rarely published. Actually looking at it with your eyes is good. I recommend that even if you think you are a good skier, you stick to the green slopes until you are actually bored with doing them, and then work up through the colours slowly. If you are a beginner, don't leave the nursery slopes until you are actually frustrated that you can't go faster.

As soon as the gradient is more than a few degrees, you will start to experience a strange acceleration as you turn into the fall line. This effect is called 'gravity'. Many skiers find it absolutely terrifying, while still trying to cover their anxieties with a cool facade. As soon as you are intimidated by the 'runaway train', your weight will come back, your posture will be compromised, and you will put an unnecessary amount of physical effort into skidding around trying to slow down. Why put yourself through it? There's no point in practising bad technique, collecting aches and pains, and falling out with the guy who suggested this 'red would be fun'.

GRADIENT: DEGREES AND PER CENT

It's very easy, when reading about the steepness or otherwise of a slope, to get mixed up between the two major systems for describing said slopeage.

It's often said that the steeper the hill, the more physical strength and technique it takes to ski it. And that's true, but as with many subjects, teachers and writers sometimes get a bit muddled about the actual physics. It does not take more strength or skill to stand still, upright on a slope, apart from the slight differences in ankle strength to hold your edges in place. It does not take more power or technique to ski straight down the fall line either, if the surface is perfect and smooth. What does take strength and ability is to make powerful enough turns to control your descent, to apply the brakes and stop, and to soak up the bumps at speed.

If you're finding it hard, it's too steep for you!

SEVEN DELUSIONS OF SKIING PEOPLE

There are quite a few things many people believe about skiing that are questionable at best, and utterly misguided at worst. Let's have some fun with that!

1. Socks for skiing must be extra thick, and especially designed for skiing. This just isn't true. Read all about it on page 39.

2. 'Getting down' a run is in any way a reflection of your skiing ability. Well, actually getting down a beginner/green run is. It means you can basically ski. Any other kind of run, you're definitely getting to the bottom, wearing your skis or not. The only question is whether you exhibited any semblance of style and panache while doing it. 'Getting down' an extreme black run is something any four-year-old can do. Acing it is all about power and control.

3. It's all about the après... There is nothing quite like hurtling through freezing mountain air to blow away a hangover. So why not go for it at the bar? After all, the more people too tired or fragile to ski in the mornings, the more fresh powder and corduroy for the rest of us!

4. All (insert local nationality here) are great at skiing. They aren't. Many people from Paris are epically rubbish at skiing, and as clueless about the basic practicalities of getting around in the snow as any other non-mountain folk. Just look at the number of them that refuse to buy winter tyres and then drive to the Alps! But make no mistake, the local locals are not just great at skiing. They are effortless at it. Like you and I are at, I don't know, breathing.

5. The fact that English is the common language of most different nationalities means that no one expects you to speak anything other than English. In English-speaking countries like the US, Canada, Australia and New Zealand, yes... and in a handful of larger French and Swiss resorts that are so popular with the Brits that the locals have mostly fled in terror, perhaps. Everywhere else, the locals will think you're incredibly rude and do their best to make your life difficult. So, do try to learn a few words!

6. There is something wrong with your equipment (and that's why you wobbled, fell down, or otherwise failed to look suitably awesome). This is very rarely the case. The only people who have stuff wrong with their equipment are the locals, who have been using the same kit every day for years, which is why it's all broken but they never have time to fix it, except maybe with glue or duct tape. And they never wobble, or fall over, or fail to look awesome.

7. There is only one sort of skiing worth considering (alpine downhill). Well, I'm sure there is a good reason for it being the most popular sort of skiing. Although I personally can't fathom what that reason is. But I definitely recommend you have a go at one of the other sorts for at least one day of your holidays. It might change your life!

CHAPTER THREE

ONWARDS & UPWARDS

SKI LIFTS AND HOW TO USE THEM

The average book on skiing tells you all about how to ski downhill in a number of different ways, but skiers experience a lot more anxiety over the mechanism of getting uphill – the ski lift. Lifts are a super well-developed way to deliver customers to the top of the slopes as quickly and efficiently as possible, but most varieties are also super intimidating to the beginner and even many intermediate skiers. Furthermore, even some competent skiers have unfortunately had lift etiquette somewhat overlooked in their learning process, and because they 'know what they're doing' they remain closed-minded and blissfully unaware of the problems they are causing to other slope users.

THE MONEY MACHINE

Skiing is a popular luxury sport, and has brought affluence to many mountain regions. One of the ways that the resort makes money out of skiers is by charging them rather a lot to use the ski lifts.

I say it's a lot of money. Of course everything's relative. And the whole system is planned rather well, from a capitalist perspective. A day on the mountain costs, per person, the same sort of money that a decent meal and a couple of drinks would be in a mid-range restaurant in the city. For a longer period, there's usually a bit of an economy of scale. A week's ski pass will probably cost much the same as a half decent suit, or a minor service on the car. If you are lucky enough to need one, a season pass for most resorts costs a fair bit to buy, but break it down into days and it's usually a bargain – the same sort of price as two weeks' passes. Over a whole winter it works out per day about the same price as a coffee in a high-street chain.

Nowadays the technology for spending your money is pretty advanced. Gone are the days of buying paper tickets. Most resorts now have an electromagnetic card that is automatically detected by the turnstile to allow you onto the lift. At the point of purchase, your photograph and name and other details will have been embedded in the data, so you can't lend your pass to anyone else. The info flashes up on a screen for the lift attendant to see. Otherwise, people would buy season passes and rent them out to guests, bringing the whole system to its knees.

It's worth mentioning at this point that the nursery slope in most resorts is free to use, and there is no need to buy a pass for whatever lift or tow is in place there. And so we begin.

ROPE TOW

As a beginner, the type of lift you will most likely encounter on day one will be one specifically designed to make life easy for the less confident, or competent, first-time skier. Some resorts even have conveyor belts you can simply step onto that will deliver you to the top of the nursery/bunny slope. More common, however, is the rope tow. It's a simple loop of rope at about waist height on an adult, so still within reach of tiny people, passing around a pulley at each end that propels it. You can join it at any point along its length, and as long as your skis are pointing in vaguely the right direction, the rope will drag you up the slope. If someone ahead of you falls and blocks your path, just let the rope slip through your gloved hands until they roll out of the way. When you arrive at the top of the slope, though, it's polite to shuffle away from the rope to leave the exit clear for the next person.

← **Elasticated button lifts are child's play, but tiny people sometimes need a hand.**

ELASTIC DRAG LIFTS

An interim solution between the rope tow and slightly more intimidating drag lifts, but very good practice for the latter, is an elasticated button lift found on many nursery slopes. The hanging poles are permanently attached to the cable, so that it's a simple matter of grabbing the next one that passes, but they have an elasticated shockcord portion that means there will never be a sudden yank as you set off. If you have ski sticks, hold them both in one hand. Then take hold of the drag thing, make sure your skis are pointed uphill, and place the plate-like bit between your legs. Hold onto it until you get to where you're going, and then hand it away and vacate the exit zone.

DRAG LIFTS – T-BAR AND BUTTON/ PLATTER

The drag lift, generally speaking, looks like a medieval torture device, and it's approached with a comparable amount of trepidation by the average beginner and many holiday skiers alike. There is really no reason for this fear, because the drag lift is really easy to use and presents no real problems for anyone on two planks. Snowboarders, on the other hand, have every reason to hate them. But that's another story.

By far the most common drag lift is the button lift, known in the US as a platter. You may already have had a chance to play on an elasticated baby version of the same on the nursery slopes, but even if you haven't, it's simple

← **Once the drag lift is towing you up the hill, relax and stay in the centre of the track. Don't worry if it jerks or accelerates or goes downhill for a bit. Don't do anything until it's time to unhook and ski off.**

enough. The clever bit is that the hanging pole is not attached to the cable. Instead it 'grabs' the cable when the skier is in position. This allows these lifts to run at quite high speeds, typically about 4m/s (13ft per second), but it can mean there's a bit of a jerk when you start.

The T-bar works in the same way, but the T part is long enough that two skiers can take the same drag, one each side of the hanging pole. This takes a modicum of organisation and communication, so I suggest you save it until you're confident. One person can easily take the T on their own, anyway.

Whichever type of drag lift it is, it can be a bit confusing at first because it's not clear what's supposed to happen. Here's what's supposed to happen:

As with any lift off the baby slopes, you'll negotiate the turnstile with your pass/ticket. Approach the drag thing, where the poles are all hanging waiting for customers, ski sticks in your less favourite hand. Now, you might pass through a little trip-trigger at shin height, or it

might all be done with lasers, but somehow the device will know you are there. Advance to the line (there's usually a line), and the next pole will sort of pop out in front of you. Don't panic, there's no rush, and calmly take hold of the metal pole and place the seat bit (plastic plate or T) behind your thighs. Don't sit down on it! Just wait, and the mechanism will after a few moments clatter into life and lock on to the cable, dragging you off up the hill.

There might be a slight tug.

Or there might be an almighty jerk. They do vary. It's never of the order that you need to be some sort of super-athlete though. To ensure that it doesn't catch you off guard, just slump back in your boots a bit. This is the one time it's a good idea on skis, but let your legs press against the back of the boots while riding drag lifts. And remember, the lift pulls you by your thighs/bottom. Relax and stand there. Don't take all the strain on your arm. There's no need.

At the other end (keep an eye out for signage to tell you when), you just need to unhook the button or T and let go of it when you can see your way to skiing or shuffling away. The exit is often a downhill off-ramp, so be ready to ski. The tow pole will carry on to go around and back to the start, so if there's anyone standing nearby, do try not to fling it at them!

CHAIR LIFTS

Chair lifts vary more than drags, but let's focus on what they have in common. You go through the turnstile. You advance to the line, perhaps passing through another automated gate of some sort. The chair comes round behind you, and you sit on it. It's not rocket science. However, there are a whole bunch of different details you can try to ignore, and a couple that you shouldn't.

Sometimes, as you advance to the correct spot, conditions throw you a curve ball. The snow can be a lot faster or slower than you were expecting, even if you took the same chair yesterday. Some chairlifts have a sort of rubber conveyor to help you to the right place. Or the approach is just made of carpet. Either sticky as hell and your skis stop dead as they hit it. Except on the days when it's icy, and you ski right off the end. None of this takes any expertise really, but pay attention to what you're doing and don't be overconfident!

Chairlifts come in many sizes, from two to six people on each chair. If it's busy, you may have to wait in line for a while to get on the lift, and to help things along it's expected that you'll fill the spaces on the chair. If there are only two in your party, don't wait it out or expect to take a chair to yourselves. The only exception to this is, if you (or they) aren't confident, it's sometimes better not to mix skiers and snowboarders

or other devices (sit-ski, scooters, etc) on the same chair. Look around you to see how things are panning out.

If it's not busy, and there are only a few of you on a wide chair, do for heaven's sake sit in the middle or evenly distributed! Nothing looks sillier than a six person chair with two people sitting at one end!

Once you've sat down safely, start thinking about the safety rail. Someone has to pull it down. It doesn't matter who, but make sure your poles are safe and your legs aren't where the rail needs to sit. Then relax and enjoy the ride, resting your skis on the footrests.

➡ **I said make sure your poles are safe, but this is different. Stops children dropping them, but still...**

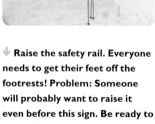

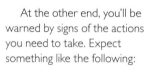

At the other end, you'll be warned by signs of the actions you need to take. Expect something like the following:

⬇ **This one is to tell you the end is in sight.**

⬇ **Raise the safety rail. Everyone needs to get their feet off the footrests! Problem: Someone will probably want to raise it even before this sign. Be ready to comply!**

ETIQUETTE

Whatever type of lift you use, there's a certain etiquette at the end too.

If you *are* next to a snowboarder, do remember they can't do much steering with their back foot out. And they can't brake at all in a straight line, so don't cut them off.

If *you* need to slow down, remember that your snowplough is wider behind you than you are. If people are shoulder to shoulder, how's that going to work?

Do not stand around in front of the lift exit messing with your poles or reading your messages, for all of the above reasons. Go away!

CABLE CAR

→ **This is the easy bit. Stand up, pushing off the chair with your fists, poles still clenched in one of them. The chair will slow down, so just push away from it.**

Personally, it terrifies me how early people raise the safety bar in Europe, especially if there are small children on the chair. I'd rather be too late and look a fool because the attendant has to stop the lift, than have someone fall off while it's still 20ft off the ground. No one ever seems to, but it still scares me...

Some mountains require that you use a cable car to access the skiing areas. The good news is, this is very easy on you. Take your skis off, and walk into the cabin with them and your poles in a bear hug. Some smaller cabins need you to put the skis in a bin on the outside – if so, do it but take your poles in with you.

↑ **Some lifts end on terrifying edifices like this one!**

↓ **Don't mess about with poles, gloves or cellphones on the chair. It is truly amazing how many people drop them.**

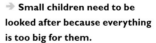

→ **Small children need to be looked after because everything is too big for them.**

HUMAN TRAFFIC AND RULES OF THE ROAD

When you first learn to ski, it's difficult to think outside of your own personal space. Controlling your own speed and not falling over is pretty much all you can mentally accommodate. As soon as you're moving downhill and surrounded by other brightly coloured people, zig-zagging around seemingly at random, the situation seems even more complicated and even quite experienced skiers can be forgiven for being a bit nervous. That's why there is an internationally recognised set of traffic rules, and they do make things clearer and easier. The official FIS guide is shown opposite. They've made it fun and child friendly, which keeps the mood light for adults, too. You may also see some local safety signage – some of that is less fluffy and inclusive.

Traditionally, the rules could be drilled down to one simple concept: the priority and right of way goes to the skier downhill. So, if you were approaching someone from above, it was your responsibility to avoid them, give them enough space, and so on. That is still true, but the FIS have gone to some trouble to de-emphasise this 'priority' statement. The problem was, skiers would only look downhill, and not check uphill when manoeuvring, joining a new run, or making a major direction change. And in that case, no matter how hard the skier above might try, sometimes a close call or even a collision would occur. As anyone who has driven a car or ridden a bicycle will know, having the right of way doesn't mean it's not a good idea to look over your shoulder before doing anything!

The FIS rules are good, but still a little basic. There are situations where the protocol isn't clear. When several runs are all converging on a single lift, for instance, there is potential for skiers approaching each other from opposite directions. There's no rule for this.

In fact the most important thing in most situations is speed control. Skiing is not all about speed unless you are racing on a closed hill, or for

↑ A complex junction where skiers approach lifts from several directions.

➜ In some resorts there is still signage that emphasises right of way more than responsible riding.

when there is no one else around. If there is any kind of human traffic, it's essential to control your speed so that you can stop at a moment's notice, or manoeuvre around others no matter what they might do without warning!

It's as well to understand that some skiers get carried away in the excitement, and imagine they are riding in the Olympic downhill when they are on a public piste with people of all ages and abilities. Others might have strayed onto a slope that is too steep for them, and are actually unable to control their speed as well as they should for everyone's safety.

It's also good to know how other snow users function. See pages 96-7 and 11 for some understanding of the behaviour of handiski, veloski, and in particular snowboarders, who have very different dynamics from those of skiers on the hill.

F/S snowkidz

10 FIS Rules for the Conduct of Skiers and Snowboarders

Rule 1: Respect for others

A skier or snowboarder must behave in such a way that he does not endanger or prejudice others.

Rule 2: Control of speed and skiing or snowboarding

A skier or snowboarder must move in control. He must adapt his speed and manner of skiing or snowboarding to his personal ability and to the prevailing conditions of terrain, snow and weather as well as to the density of traffic.

Rule 3: Choice of route

A skier or snowboarder coming from behind must choose his route in such a way that he does not endanger skiers or snowboarders ahead.

Rule 4: Overtaking

A skier or snowboarder may overtake another skier or snowboarder above or below and to the right or to the left provided that he leaves enough space for the overtaken skier or snowboarder to make any voluntary or involuntary movement.

Rule 5: Entering, starting and moving upwards

A skier or snowboarder entering a marked run, starting again after stopping or moving upwards on the slopes must look up and down the slopes that he can do so without endangering himself or others.

Rule 6: Stopping on the piste

Unless absolutely necessary, a skier or snowboarder must avoid stopping on the piste in narrow places or where visibility is restricted. After a fall in such a place, a skier or snowboarder must move clear of the piste as soon as possible.

Rule 7: Climbing and descending on foot

A skier or snowboarder either climbing or descending on foot must keep to the side of the piste.

Rule 8: Respect for signs and markings

A skier or snowboarder must respect all signs and markings.

Rule 9: Assistance

At accidents, every skier or snowboarder is duty bound to assist.

Rule 10: Identification

Every skier or snowboarder and witness, whether a responsible party or not, must exchange names and addresses following an accident.

www.fis-snowkidz.com

FIS ©2010

← **Beginners taking their first tentative steps are unlikely to be a hazard.**

BEGINNERS

There isn't really a problem with beginners, which will no doubt be good news if you are one! Beginners ski slowly and predictably and rarely cause anyone any trouble. Sometimes, because they're not so familiar with the mountain environment, they stand around in some odd places. Like right in front of a lift exit. But to be honest, because they don't go anywhere too committing, even that isn't a problem.

SNOWBOARDERS

Snowboarders were viewed with suspicion from the moment they arrived on the slopes in the 1980s. First they weren't allowed on the lifts – and some might argue that they still should not be – and then later they were made to wear leashes in case the board, not having brakes like skis, got away from them. Most of the suspicion and regulation derived from skiers just not understanding how snowboards function, but there's a snowflake of truth to the argument – snowboards are much harder to control and to stop on the piste than skis. Snowboarders sit down a lot, because standing still is a superhuman feat on a snowboard unless you are on flat ground, and no one wants to be on flat ground on a snowboard.

Boarders find it much more difficult to use ski lifts than skiers, mostly because they were designed for skiers. It is better for skiers not to try to share a chair lift with them, because their boards tend to point across the chair, and they struggle to ride off the lift at the other end. In particular, skiers should understand that a snowboard cannot brake without turning sideways. So don't cut in front of a boarder who is trapped between two other people!

INTERMEDIATE SKIERS

Intermediate skiers are a potential nightmare for many reasons. Some of them think they are much better skiers than they are, with the inevitable consequences. But these consequences usually impact on them, not others. But the thing most inters have in common is that they are still learning pretty fast every time they go skiing. I know in my case, on a skiing holiday I would improve rapidly all week. And then the next holiday, I'd have regressed 90% of the way back again. Because intermediates are busy improving, they have even less awareness of what's going on around them than beginners, and hence they are the cause of most traffic problems on the slopes.

EXPERTS

I think everyone already knows the trouble with experts – it's that anyone who thinks they are an expert, or says so anyway, probably isn't one. A real pro is nothing to worry about and is either wonderful

← **Snowboarders have a tendency to travel sideways. Beware.**

⬆ **Scooters and other weird stuff is difficult to second guess.**

⬆ **Monoskiers ride like skiers but in many respects (stopping) are like snowboarders.**

⬇ **The freeskier looks either like an alien or a hooligan but is probably very safe.**

to watch and learn from, or unlikely to cross your path unless you are one too, but the self-confessed expert is too fast, too loud, and too on the same blue slope as people who just don't need that.

WEIRD AND WONDERFUL

There's an increasing smattering of monoskiers, veloskis, sno-scoots and other weird stuff I don't know the name for on the slopes these days, but 99% of the snow users are either skiers or snowboarders. The trouble with these minorities then, is that they are such a rarity that no one really knows what to do with them. It's not clear what they're up to, or which way they're going to turn!

FREESKIERS

These guys, usually teenagers, embody the attitude that snowboarders used to be stereotyped with... that of the hoody-wearing hooligan. They probably aren't hooligans, they probably are better skiers than most, and they are probably less likely to be drunk than the older folk on the hill! Actually I think there's a lot to be learnt from the freeskiers...

MIXED ABILITIES

The trouble with mixed ability groups is that ultimately, we are all skiing alone. It's fun to swish down the hill with someone who is about the same speed and confidence as yourself. Equally, none of us would progress if it wasn't for the inspiration and guidance of better or more experienced skiers. But what happens in a mixed ability group is, someone is always saying 'Come with us to this (steeper) slope. Go on... you'll be all right!'

SWISHING AND SWOOPING

We have all seen advanced skiers descending the slopes in a series of uniform Ss, rhythmically rising, falling and turning for all the world as if this was a natural thing to do. But you don't see cyclists, for instance, going down hills this way, or any other vehicle for that matter. Or walkers. So what's it all about?

A bicycle has brakes. A person on foot, too, can slow themselves down or stop quite easily. But for a skier to control his or her speed, they have to turn across the fall line in order to get some velocity vectored across the hill (see page 16) and stop just accelerating *down*

the hill. Each turn, too, scrubs off a little bit of speed because of the added friction and bending the skis.

It is within our power to snowplough or sideslip all the way down the hill, but this is a) exhausting, b) dull, and c) does not work in deeper snow. So once you are skiing in, broadly speaking, parallel mode, it will become necessary to keep making turns.

How wide the turns need to be in order to feel in control is determined by the speed and steepness of the slope and the confidence and state of mind of the skier. It might be safe to point

PROGRESSING THE TURNS

This is the part where I tell you about a whole bunch of things without telling you why, or how to do them. But I think it's best to go into the basic technique section with some understanding of where we are going with it. So this is the order in which the different ways of turning are usually learned, and a little about each one of them. Don't worry, we'll look at the actual mechanics of how to do them a bit later on.

The wedge turn or snowplough is executed by moving the skis into, surprisingly, a wedge shape. The skier can alter the stance, the pressure, and the angle of the edges with the legs, but there is no complex timing or edge changes to worry about. With this one position, a four-year old can descend almost any slope. Both skis are on the big toe edge the whole time.

I should point out that the word 'christie', while historically interesting, is kind of outdated and is rarely used by modern skiers except to differentiate very subtle differences between turns. And only then if they've actually heard of it...

WEDGE CHRISTIES

They begin like the wedge turn but the inside leg switches edges once the turn has started. The inside ski is rolled off the big toe edge onto its little toe edge. As it does so, it should come into line with the outside ski.

STEM CHRISTIE

This is a manoeuvre that is rarely taught these days except as an illustration of inefficient movement, but it's surprising how many skiers you will see doing it without

ever having been shown how. The principle is that one ski is 'stemmed' (tail swept out à la wedge) and then the second ski brought into line, but with both skis working their inside edges throughout, rather than the turn being initiated in snow plough mode.

STEP TURN

This turn can either be converging or diverging but involves a lift and step of one ski. Edge changes can occur before, after or during the step. So although it's often seen as a learner progression, it actually opens up a whole world of improvisation. For this reason, it's seen in racing quite often, but not so much in recreational skiing.

PARALLEL TURN

Simultaneous weight shift and edge changes while the skis remain parallel are what we associate with these turns, but actually a deliberately staggered release and edge change is very common among high functioning skiers. Since the introduction of modern sidecut skis the concept of both skis being perfectly in unison has ceased to be the ultimate expression of skiing excellence.

SUPER PARALLEL

Now that it's no longer de rigueur to ski oldschool, advanced skiers use a mixture of all of the above techniques, and at the limit they use whatever works best for the situation. The expert skier will not feel any shame at throwing in a wedge of a step if that gets the job done, and as we will show later on, the modern carving turn is very rarely truly parallel.

straight down the fall line, keep the skis flat, and not do any braking at all. However, it doesn't have to be much of a hill before most of us feel a lot better shifting from one edge to another, just to feel that little bit more feedback from the skis, and to keep the body 'awake'. Sometimes the upper body is quite still but the legs are just swishing side to side from the hips.

As the slopes get steeper, it may become necessary to hold onto the edges longer and harder, so as to stop the skis from accelerating to a frightening speed. The skier is still very much descending in the fall line, but is carving constantly to and fro across it.

Extreme skiers occasionally put themselves in a situation where they cannot garner enough grip to traverse across the face of the hill, because it is so steep or icy. At this level they often end up descending in a series of sideslips, jumping 180° to face the other way instead of actually making turns, until they can get to a part of the mountain that is less insane and aim downhill once more.

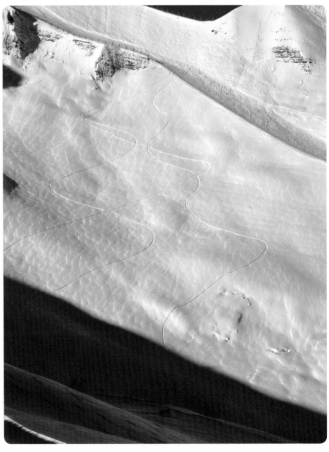

As the slope gets steeper still, the skier starts to spend most of the time carving turns to kill the speed, and as soon as one turn is finished, another begins. These turns can be quite wide now and leave spectacular gouging trails on any fresh snow on the mountain.

There comes a point for most of us where we are no longer confident to point the skis down the fall line or strong enough to hold a long slow turn. At this point we begin to turn as quickly as possible to aim across the hill at an angle that controls the speed. We psyche ourselves up, and make another turn to traverse the other way. There should be alarm bells ringing now about whether this run was a good idea.

CHAPTER FOUR
MANOEUVRES

Sideslipping is arguably the most important skill for a skier to learn after the snowplough (wedge, pizza) and certainly a fundamental part of learning most of the manoeuvres that come after. You might need to attempt it on a slightly steeper part of the hill, since going sideways on the nursery slopes doesn't really work out.

Start by standing with the skis across the fall line. Since you are not currently sideslipping, this means you already know how to control your skis. Or the slope isn't steep enough. We shall see. As an exercise, move your hips uphill to dig in your edges even more. That's just so that you get the feel for how this all works. Now, move them down the hill until the edges release and the skis start to slip. You can stop yourself immediately by returning your hips to a position uphill from your feet.

If you release the edge too much, by letting the hips move too far downhill, the sideslip will initially be effortless since the bases are flat to the hill, but there's a danger that the downhill edges start to pick up snow and might trip you.

If at all possible, look down the hill as you practise, not at your boots! This will help you to avoid the most common problem, which is...

Do not lean up the slope with your body. As with most skiing skills, it's important that your centre of gravity is over your skis. Move your hips across the skis to control how much edge you apply, but do not lean or bend your torso up the fall line as this leads to a loss of balance.

It's at this point that you'll realise that where your weight is positioned along the skis, and to some extent the pressure you may be applying by twisting your upper body, can make your tips slide downhill faster or slower than the tails of your skis. So experiment with shifting forward and aft, and apply foot and leg steering forces until you are confident you can control your descent. It really is quite subtle stuff, so just *thinking* you want the tip to slide a bit more is sometimes enough!

Now that you can slide and stop, slide and stop, it's not a huge mental leap to realise that the same principle can be applied during a turn or traverse. How much you grip the snow and direct your speed forwards, or sideslip and 'spill' the energy down the slope, is entirely under your control.

The modern way to practise this is fairly universally called 'braquage' or sometimes spelled 'bracquage'. Braquage is the French word for 'steering', which makes perfect sense, although it's hardly the French skier's first choice of turning method. Perhaps they were just sick of hearing about 'telemark' and 'christiania'. To many it sounds as if it should mean 'brakeage' though, which would make much more sense since it's a speed-control exercise not a steering one. Perhaps that's why it's been adopted by so many English speakers. The French word for 'to brake' is 'freiner'.

Braquage is also the French word for 'stick-up' or armed robbery. Not sure that helps.

BRACQUAGE

1

2

3

4

5

6

STEP AND STEM TURNS

The step turn is sometimes necessary. Cross-country skiers use it on skis that simply don't edge very well. Occasionally a skier finds one plank blocked by a piece of terrain and can't make a turn without lifting and moving it. And it's a useful exercise to keep reminding oneself that the skis don't have to stay firmly planted on the ground.

Usually the step turn is taught by using a snowplough or wedge to turn into the fall line with control over speed, and then all you have to do is step the inside ski quickly into a parallel position to accelerate down the hill.

The rarely taught stem turn (or stem christie) is slightly different. This time the ski is not usually stepped, but swept into place, which is more graceful and teaches better edge control as the skier progresses towards making parallel turns. There are two ways to make this turn, converging or diverging.

CONVERGING STEM

As the skier traverses through the fall line, the uphill ski is swept around to point more downhill, forming a wedge shape a little like applying a snowplough. The second, downhill ski is then brought around to parallel again.

DIVERGING STEM

In this exercise, the downhill ski is turned first, and then the second, uphill ski is brought into line.

What both of these exercises do, as well as being jolly useful for managing the skis independently in complex turns and difficult terrain, is familiarise the skier with controlling the edges of the two skis independently. During the sideslipping exercise, it becomes clear that moving the hips across the skis will transition them from one edge to the other. But to change the edge of one ski only cannot be done with the hips. Since the ankles are fairly firmly locked by the boots in the lateral plane, the only remaining joint we can use is the knee.

You may see a lot of skiers making turns with a slight convergence or divergence while attempting to ski parallel. This isn't because they are practising the exercises per se, but usually because they have slight alignment issues and so the skis are constantly trying to turn apart or together. Rather than addressing the root cause, the skier is simply allowing the skis to skid a little in order to keep skiing with this slight offset. It would be better to fix the posture or look at adjusting the boots or bindings to address it.

POLES APART

At first examination it's hard to see what poles are really all about. Beginners assume they are for propulsion, but soon discover there are better ways of doing this, like skating. Early on we learn to use them for support and to stop ourselves slip-sliding away, but again, this isn't absolutely necessary once a skier is confident at using the edges of the skis. So what are they for?

When you watch an expert skier planting the pole at the beginning of each turn and then swooping around it, you'd be forgiven for thinking that it's acting as some sort of pivot or lever. And it can do – see page 78 for a beginner pole strategy. But the confident downhiller does not commit any weight to the pole. It's more of a tool to engage the upper body in the language of the turn. A subtle and a powerful one. Because it's amazing how a deft point and flick on the downhill side can change for the better how your body addresses the hill, once you begin to ski parallel.

When you do anything physical, it's all about expectation and feedback. You feel what is going on, and compare it to prior experience, and adjust accordingly. When making parallel turns, there is a key moment as you being to change edges when there is very little feedback through your legs. The skis are flat on the snow and accelerating, you're almost in freefall. Well, it feels that way, anyway. The pole, at that moment, is your third point of contact and gives you vital information. The other source of information is your eyes. By pointing the pole, you lead your ocular sense to focus on the turning point and this helps a lot at the moment of reduced physical input.

First of all we need to talk about arms. Many people find it natural to ski with their arms out in front of them, or in a sort of 'A' shape, but it's better to adopt a curled-in hand position. This keeps the hands in front of the body for safety, and encourages the movement of the poles to be made with the wrists, without swinging the arms. If you wave your arms about, it leads to upper body rotation that unbalances everything. We need to keep everything neat and tidy and quiet.

Normally, one makes a turn towards the downhill side when skiing across the hill. If you were to reach forward with the arm on this side, you'd be turning your body the wrong way. We need to turn the torso to face *down* the fall line. So just flick the pole forward with the downhill hand only, and then turn the body to face it.

As you attack steeper slopes, the pole plant needs to become more positive. Swing the pole forward with the wrist, making sure your arms are still in the O shape, keeping the poles angled outwards. Plant the pole, but don't stab it into the snow so that your hand has to 'pole vault' over it – the intention is to keep the hands still and not wave the arms up and down. As the tip of the pole is swept back past the hips, the opposite wrist will already be flicking the other pole forward for the next turn. Timing is everything!

⬆ In this sequence you can see how the pole is extended using the wrist. The skier has already committed to the turn and the pole is planted just before the skis go flat to the hill. As the left pole comes back, the right pole is already extended for the next turn.

PARALLEL TURNS

For many skiers, being able to descend the hill making smooth parallel turns is the pinnacle of skiing achievement. As mentioned elsewhere, it has long been traditional to progress from the snowplough or wedge, through step and stem turns, finally to arrive at a point where the skis can carve together through the snow. As you may also have read, this is a rather outdated concept, but ski parallel we shall, for the moment at least.

If you learned to ski on fairly straight skis (not many people do these days, but it's entirely possible), then making parallel turns relied on having the body language to unweight the skis and turn them a little so that as they power up again, they will bend sufficiently to carve into the turn. Just the act of standing on the skis does bend them, and even

the straightest of downhill skis still have *some* sidecut, so it doesn't take much. But it's much easier to learn on modern skis with a big sidecut. Because you really don't have to do anything much.

Don't get me wrong. You still need to go to ski school and learn all these other good things first. If only so that you can deal with things when your first attempts at parallel don't work out as planned! But turning the modern ski is not the black art that it was thirty odd years ago when I was first in ski school.

Ski instructors are very good at taking us through the drills that will lead naturally to correct technique without our necessarily realising what we are doing, or why. When it comes to books, it's a bit more difficult, since reading and inwardly digesting this sort of information

↑ **Moving the skis onto their edge invokes a turn. The inside ski will naturally move forward as that knee tends to bend more.**

often leads to over-thinking it. I've noticed that most of the books on skiing technique talk about foot steering, and thigh (or leg) steering, and I too may make mention of it, but... usually they don't properly explain what these things mean, and they fail to mention that the skis will turn without either of these two forms of steering, just by putting them on edge. How are they put on edge? Well, you can already do it.

WEIGHT SHIFT

As explained on page 102, the skis can be edged both together by shifting the hips across the feet, or individually by shifting one or other knee to either side as well. You've used this to do every other turn and exercise in the progression, so you shouldn't have to think too much about it now. The fact is, if you lean the skis onto their right-hand edge they'll turn right, and the same the other way. As long as you actually are moving, anyway! So, how to put this into practice?

I have cajoled and ranted already about the importance of not tackling slopes that are too steep for you, and never is it more important than when trying to make your first parallel turns. The good thing is, parallel carving does not slow you down as much as wedging, brushing or skidding the skis through the snow, so the slightest of slopes is sufficient for practising. Just point the skis down the hill, and roll them smoothly onto one edge. You can just stay in this position and make a J turn, if the slope is wide enough.

If you try to practise on a steeper slope, you'll probably succeed in making the turn. However, the further you turn across the slope the more intimidating it becomes to lean down the hill to turn the skis back into the fall line. After a while, you'll be OK with this, but for now try somewhere gentle.

Once the turn is happening to your satisfaction, try not to finish the J, but instead turn your head and torso back towards the fall line, and roll the skis onto the opposite edge. In this way, you can sweep back and forth across the fall line, and finish off with a J turn or snowplough when it's time to stop.

THE CORRIDOR

It's helpful to think of skiing down a narrow corridor – this doesn't mean you need to practise on a narrow track, but imagine a corridor just a few metres wide, and try to make your turns symmetrical within

that. Make the turns as long and smooth as you can. If you try to traverse and then turn quickly, you will skid the back of the skis and lose control. Just make very long, narrow Ss along the fall line. If it feels too fast, go somewhere less steep!

NOT REALLY PARALLEL

Don't think too much about being parallel. Think more about keeping the skis on edge and equally weighted. To do this, you'll have to bend your knees differing amounts (because your legs are leaning one way), and all kinds of different things will be going on. The truth is that unless you are on a very straight type of ski that you've found in a museum, or a giant slalom or racing ski of some kind, the skis will not be pointing the same way during the turn. This is because as they are going around quite a small circle, and the modern skiing stance is quite wide, the skis are describing quite different arcs, as can be seen looking at many carving skiers.

FEET POSITION

Another thing you will notice is that as you invoke more lean and make tighter turns happen, the inside knee is more bent and tends to shunt forward in relation to the other knee. This is normal and you shouldn't mind it. In order to remain in a functional and balanced position with this amount of knee bend, the inside boot tends also to move forward so your skis are no longer side by side like the skiers of old. That's OK too. Let it happen.

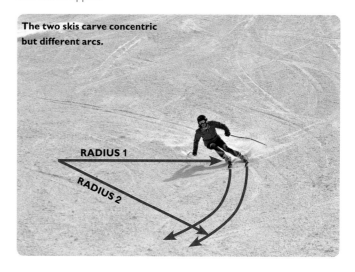

The two skis carve concentric but different arcs.

RADIUS 1

RADIUS 2

STOPPING LIKE YOU MEAN IT

↑ **Super-aggressive hockey stop.**

Now that you've got the parallel thing down, it's time to think about stopping in a different way. There's still a place for the snowplough or wedge stop. When there's no space either side of you, and you have to stop without turning. And the J turn is still a useful concept too, because we don't want to shower everyone with snow and ice crystals every time we stop to look at a pretty view. This can cause considerable upset, especially if they have their camera out.

But there comes a time when you urgently need to throw the anchors out, and there's nothing for it but to skid to a halt like a victorious Olympic champion. Or, maybe you just really want to! This move is sometimes called the 'hockey stop'. If you grew up skating on ice, you'll probably see why. If you think hockey is a game played with a ball on a field, just move along.

To do the hockey stop, you need to be basically au fait with parallel turning. It's also pretty handy to be good at the side slipping exercise discussed earlier, especially the subtle weight shifts that keep the two ends of the skis going down the hill at the same rate. If you 'spin out' you will find yourself going downhill almost as fast as you were before,

only backwards, and we aren't quite ready to do that yet!

It's a matter of making a turn into the fall line, but without a religious adherence to keeping those edges slip-free. Use your edge control to allow the skis to drift. Because it is an inefficient sort of turn, you don't carry a lot of forward speed through it, and most of the speed is retained down the fall line, albeit sideways. Now is the time to crank on more and more edge, leaning the body up the fall line. As the brakes come on, you'll feel a lot of compression in the knees and hips. Try to soak it up – it can get bumpy! Resist the tendency to break at the waist, since this will apply too much edge to the skis and maybe jump them out of the snow.

If you come to a halt with this much lean, you'll fall down. It's up to you to feather out the braking edges as you come to a stop, and allow the final bit of momentum to carry you upright again. It's too much to think about in a couple of seconds, but you have all the components of this move in your toolbox. It's just a matter of putting them together.

Remember that you can also stop by using the J turn, as described on page 82, which is a lot less aggressive and snow-showering than the

↓ **J turn.**

hockey stop. If you are going fast and making carved turns, you may have so much momentum that you actually turn back up the hill before coming to rest. So that you don't stop and then slide away backwards, be ready to step into a safe position across the fall line as you stop.

↓ **Parallel into smooth stop.**

SKIDDING AND CARVING

Many skiers make most of their turns by skidding the ski around. The ski, especially the tail part, is sliding sideways to some degree as well as travelling forwards. While this is an essential skill for the skier, and indeed we are taught to practise it deliberately (see braquage, page 102), it is important to understand the differences between skidding and carving, and to switch between these two modes at will.

← **Ending the turn with the skis oversteering and skidding sideways before engaging for the next turn.**

Expert skiers, and those who learned to ski using skis with very little shape, tend to carve as the preferred mode. The ski will only be skidded to make an urgent redirect, and then the skier will return to carving. The carving skier controls the speed with the line that they take on the hill, not by skidding. The skidding ski does not deal well with bumps and variations in the snow and is prone to catching an edge, making involuntary direction changes and even precipitating a fall. The physical effort of trying to control the skis and soak up the bumps

SIDECUT IRONY

There are a set of conflicting issues here. One reason for the fairly rapid introduction of 'shaped' skis during the 1990s was the fact that expert skiers recognised the potential of snowboards. With extra width and massively more sidecut than the skis of the time, snowboards were not only riding effortlessly in deep powder, but they were capable of carving almost perfect arcs on the hard pack. I say capable – many snowboarders were and still are skittering around on the piste, descending the slope in a series of noisy, scraping, effortful sideslips. The irony is that now, with the almost universal adoption of these heavily sidecut skis, many skiers are now doing the same thing. Modern planks have made it very easy to ski well. And very easy to ski badly.

and shocks is disproportionate to the rate of travel. The carving ski is a good deal better at riding over or through these transient negative conditions, faster and more smoothly.

This is not to say that skidding is bad. What's bad is not being able to stop doing it. Increasingly, top racing athletes are using aggressive skidding strategies to get down the hill better, and extreme skiers too rely on getting sideways now and again. But it's best to think of it as something to do when needed, not all the time.

Two words that crop up a lot with modern skiers are 'slarve' and 'stivot'. And just like the stem christies of old, there's always a little bit of 'regional variation' in how they are defined.

Slarve (sliding carve) is usually used to describe what some skiers call a McConkey turn, after the late great Shane McConkey, one of the pioneers of modern

extreme skiing. The skis are progressively skidded, usually in the latter or closing stages of the turn, primarily as a speed-control strategy. It's also quite spectacular.

The stivot (steering pivot) is a rapid redirect, not much more than a twist before the skis resume gripping and carving, and is used primarily by racers to get tighter than the traditionally executable radius early on in the turn. Their intent is quite different – slowing down is the last thing they want to do.

These moves, which might be called 'bad form' by oldschool skiers, have come about partly through the introduction of rockered skis for powder and the need to overcome the huge turning radii of slalom and GS skis. To hit them hard and ride away takes a lot of courage and athleticism, but there is also a place for a cheeky slide in everyday piste skiing.

Skidding generally happens more in the tail part of the ski, causing *oversteer* or an increase in the rate of turn. It occurs typically for beginners when the weight is back and the skis relatively flat. More confident skiers feel it with the weight forward on moderately edged skis. A skidding skier throws a trail of loose snow to the outside of the turn, whereas a hard-carving one leaves a line gouged in the snow as if with a knife.

CHAPTER FIVE

BODY LANGUAGE IN SKIING

STEERING AND BALANCE

There is no single factor in the art of skiing that is quite so important as this. Apart from snow – no, we can manage without that, with roller-skis, grass skis, artificial slopes, poor imitations of the real thing that they are. I guess skis, then, are quite important too. But body language, yes. It's important.

The usual way to learn this is to follow your instructor's lead, and mimic his or her body motions. Humans are actually very good at this, and it works very well. But since there are a number of different components to the swishing and swooping that is skiing, I thought it would be nice to break them down into some chunks that are manageable to think about. Some people learn by doing, some by watching, some by listening. And by virtue of the fact that you're still here, some by reading!

CENTRE OF GRAVITY/MASS

I'm going to use the two phrases interchangeably, because I can't imagine skiing in zero gravity happening anytime soon. I think it helps to be vaguely aware of where your centre of mass lies. People vary quite a bit in body shape, but generally the centre of gravity is somewhere just behind the navel, or a little lower. For women it's generally a tiny bit lower than in men. Once you are wearing your boots and skis, this point shifts down a bit more. Alpine skis and boots are really quite heavy! So we are looking at somewhere in the crotch area, perhaps. Your perineum, to give it its medical name.

Now that you know where it is, it's a really good idea to think about how you are using it. Most of the time it needs to be above your feet, so that you don't fall over, or at least give your abs an unnecessary workout. Skiing does that quite enough as it is! In a dynamic sense, when turning and so forth, of course you may end up leaning over a fair bit and, just like riding a bicycle, relying on the centrifugal force and grip on the ground to keep everything from crashing down. But generally, keep your centre of gravity above your feet especially in the front-to-back plane.

Flexing the ankles and bending the knees will bring it forward a little, but that's OK. This is one reason why skis are longer in front than behind. Most importantly, try not to let your weight get behind the bindings. This can happen if you bend at the waist, which makes you stick your bottom out or hang back in your boots.

MY NUMBER ONE RULE FOR ALL UPSTANDING SPORTS – DON'T BREAK AT THE WAIST! RULE 2 – UNLESS YOU REALLY WANT TO!

FOOT AND LEG STEERING

There is no doubt that these things exist. But when you first try to ski parallel, your instinct is to try to twist the skis in the snow by brute force, and it doesn't really work very well. In combination with the other skills that an instructor will walk you through, these efforts can be the fine control you need to control your skis. But I promise that if you are skiing down a hill, and you try simply to twist your feet using any selection of muscles at your disposal, not much will happen.

RAILING THE SKIS

On modern skis you can, in fact, make parallel turns with no skills whatsoever, simply by tilting the skis. But equally, if you turn simply by rolling the skis onto their edges with no additional body language, the radius of the turn will be dictated entirely by the natural shape of the skis and this doesn't always suit the terrain or the turn you need to make. So before you go too fast, too steep or too bumpy, it's useful to consider some of the more skilful body language that can be employed.

PROJECTION

By projection I mean driving your hips forward and across the skis. The across part puts the power into your leg tilt and forces those edges into the snow. The forward part, in conjunction with sinking into your bended knees (see the next bit) is pushing your shins against the front of the boots, which, if you think about it, bends (most of) the ski area that is in front of your legs. It feels like launching your centre of gravity in the direction indicated by your pole plant.

SINK AND PRESS

You have to sink into your skis for two reasons. The first is that when you arrive at your chosen limit of sinkage, you will pressurise the skis and bend them more. The second is to give yourself some room to move when you want to unweight them to change edges. It is this rising and sinking action, coming mainly from the knees, that allows the skier to recover smoothly from a turn with the skis bending and gouging a tight radius turn, through a phase where they are flat and going straight, into the next turn in the opposite direction.

PEDALLING

As we've seen elsewhere there is a natural tendency to shunt the inside knee forward as you lean into the turn, and the outside leg will be straighter than the inside one, although not completely straight. This makes perfect sense, because you are leaning over and the one side of you is closer to the ground than the other. The outside

ski is also going around the outside of the bend, so it needs to go faster than the inside one but with slightly less curvature. The inside ski therefore needs to be bent more, so the greater drive of the inside leg against the front of the boot gives us that. You are, sort of, pushing it into the turn with your hips/legs/feet. As you straighten up and then drop into the next turn, this leg position reverses, and you'll get the idea that it's very much like pedalling a bicycle. Practise making fairly short, narrow and rhythmic turns, skiing in a corridor as suggested before, and you will be able to feel this pedalling action and optimise it so that you're aware of the pressure you're putting into each ski.

SMOOTHNESS

Doing all four of these body movements is important to get an efficient and powerful turn, but you must do them smoothly. If you try to edge the skis by throwing your hips over one way, your upper body

➡ **A small mistake can often escalate into a bigger one, as the raised arm to fix a balance problem raises the centre of mass and centrifugal force, pulling the skier upright and possibly even over the skis.**

will be out of balance, probably some frantic arm waving will ensue, and the skis won't settle into a progressive turn, instead bouncing and skittering in a direction that their designer didn't allow for. The same problem exists if you stamp your feet instead of pedalling smoothly à la bicyclette, or bounce up and down like a deranged jack in the box! Ease into the movements and as you feel the pressure build in the skis, match that pressure with your legs until it's time to let the stored energy in the skis spring back at you as progressively as you built it up.

GRACE UNDER PRESSURE

Through the actions that you take in order to make turns, you'll become aware of the pressure that you pump into your skis, but there is additional pressure that comes not from your body language but from the snow itself. Snow varies in density and fluffiness as we've seen, but it's always to some degree compressible, squashy stuff. However, as you drive into the more serious turns, you are initially pushing the ski into the snow towards the outside of the turn, and as you compact it more it resists more, until your centrifugal force is pressing the base of the ski against an increasingly unyielding wall of snow. So it's clear to see that the pressure is going to increase almost exponentially in this type of scenario.

If you allow the combined pressure (your leg push/projection + snow build-up reaction) to become too much, one of two things will happen: a) your legs/core may collapse under the strain, or b) the skis may skip up out of their grooves and skid away from you. Or some combination of the two!

⬆ The skier has put too much pressure on the outside ski, resulting in the leg becoming extended as it skids away. Furthermore all the load is now on the inside one!

⬇ This skier no longer has any engagement with the snow with the outside ski, and so the outside leg has therefore pushed out straight.

SKI FLEX

The ski, when you bend it, is storing potential energy very much like a coiled spring, and the modern ski design incorporates technology to make it very good at this, including enormous strength, appropriate elasticity, and optimised damping. When you stop bending it, it springs back. Ideally this will happen in a way that assists your transition to the next turn, but if you don't unweight it progressively, this energy may come back to bite you.

GOING STEEP

I go on and on about how you should not ski slopes that are too steep for your ability or current state of mind or sobriety, but eventually this is the challenge that many of us seek. So, we'd better be prepared...

WHAT IS STEEP TO YOU?

It's quite difficult to make good judgements about steepness. That's one reason why resorts have so much signage to try to guide skiers into good choices. Looking at a hill from afar, it takes a fair bit of

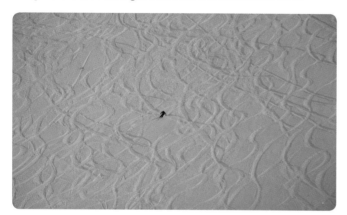

experience to figure out the real implications. Let's say this. 25° is steep to many people. 35° is steep to most people. 45° plus is madness, expert-only territory. But of course icy or other difficult conditions can ramp up the severity of any given gradient. So proceed with caution.

COMMITMENT TO CARVING

Skidding has its place, as we'll see, but it is untidy and it's hard work. It's also rather difficult to control on steep or icy surfaces. As we've discussed somewhere else, the expert skier actually skis on their downhill edge, except when traversing. And even when travelling across the slope, you have to transition onto the downhill edges of the skis when you want to turn into the fall line. When the slope is very steep, there's a problem with that which isn't hard to see.

A firm pole plant and the dynamic balance that comes from turning will help, of course, but it's still a bit of a brave move. When the going gets steep, the tough get committed to carving close to the fall line. And that does mean speed... but constant speed is actually less scary, if you're in control, than rapid acceleration and braking.

⬇ **Don't hurl yourself headlong, but do try constantly to project your body towards the fall line.**

FEAR OF THE FALL LINE

If you are afraid of the speed, then you'll tend to hesitate to turn into the fall line. This leads to more fear, because you are traversing and tiring your legs killing speed by sideslipping, and this makes the acceleration that comes with any impending turn all the more intimidating. As the skis run away with you, the first instinct is to slam on the brakes again, and now you're right back where you started but facing the other way. If, however, you just keep on carving, the speed will be pretty much constant, and it's not too scary to make the edge change between each turn because it is a) quick, and b) happens during the most traversey part of the sequence. So keep it tight, and try to ski down a 2m (6ft) wide corridor, instead of getting sucked into a big (and scary to get out of) traverse.

⬇ **Concentrate on keeping your hips turned to point down the hill at all times.**

GAINING CONFIDENCE

Most skiers struggle in the steeps because they lack confidence. And most people's response to that is to a) hit the brakes, and b) 'get in the back seat', meaning let the bodyweight shift back. Neither of these things help your skiing, so it seems to be going badly, and because of this an ever shrinking comfort zone is a constant problem.

First, don't tackle the most severe steeps. Work your way up. Second, as with mogul skiing (see page 178), pick somewhere with a flat or uphill run-out to practise attacking the steep. Then you aren't intimidated, because the end is in sight. Third, understand the difference between controlling your speed by braking, and controlling it by turning. In the former case, the hill is constantly steep, and you're fighting gravity with limited resources of strength and energy. In the later scenario, the hill is less steep when you are carving across it, and the skis are slowed down by bending and carving. So, you can fight against gravity or use it. Tough choice. See the graph on page 86.

USE YOUR POLES

You've read the pole plant section (see page 106), but never is it more important than in the steeps. Plant the pole a metre (3ft) downhill from your skis. This will give you confidence, and help you to throw your weight down the hill. Try to project your body into the fall line, keeping your hips facing downhill at all times. Keep your centre of gravity moving onwards and your hips ahead of your heels, because if the weight comes back, the skis will push straight on, depriving you of both directional and speed control. Keep your weight pressing forward and towards the fall line, and this will provide you with the right steering and edge control, making the skis bite in and flatten out at the right times.

CHAPTER SIX

OTHER WAYS

SNOWBLADES

Salomon. Moves to call the sport anything else have not met with widespread acceptance, but they are often called skiblades, or skiboards. Confusing, I know...

The thing is, since snowblades were invented, and were 'crazy short' at around one metre or less, recreational skis have got shorter too. So to a person used to skis in the 140cm range, a slightly shorter plank doesn't seem radical, or necessary. But there are some differences that make them appealing.

Snowblades don't generally have the complex sidecut of modern skis. The bindings can be simpler and lighter. This, and the lack of the need for poles, makes them light and easy to transport. You can just dangle them over your shoulder on a leash or stick them in a moderately sized backpack.

Blades are just short enough that they are easy to turn without normal skiing body language. A twist of the legs will implement a rapid change of direction, without the need for carving or aggressive edging. This makes it incredibly easy to learn and to progress rapidly to steeper slopes. Most people don't need lessons, since it feels so natural, especially if you have any experience of roller blading, skiing, snowboarding or ice skating; it is a very natural cross-over. The disadvantage is that you can end up on slopes that require more edge length to get any grip, but the physical attrition of sideslipping down on blades is much less than on even short carving skis.

AREN'T THEY JUST SHORT SKIS?

Snowblades do come in quite varied lengths and widths. Some narrow ones do feel like skis, but many wider ones are like having tiny snowboards on your feet. Choosing the right length depends on your personal style as well as height and weight.

Blades vary from about 75 to 150cm in length and are generally made with a solid wood core and variety of shapes, just like snowboards.

Snowblades (skiblades) became popular in the '90s, at a time when skiers were looking for a way to have a more casual experience. When we first saw people on the slopes with skis that were barely longer than their boots, everyone said it was crazy and would never catch on. Like everything new (snowboarding suffered the same thing) the skiing traditionalists felt it was reckless and dangerous and that you couldn't possibly be in control on blades.

While they are known generically as snowblades at the time of writing, this was originally a trademark of the ski manufacturer

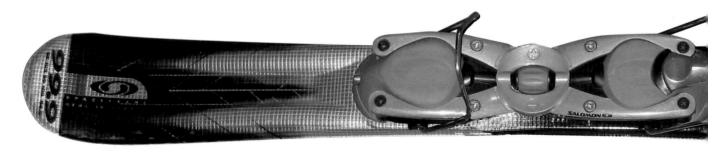

When people who can already ski get onto really short planks they sometimes complain that the blades are not very directional. And of course they are not speed machines. The secret is to stand up more and not try to attack the front half of the rail with weight projection – you can't get so far forward because there just isn't anything there. The technique is much more like skating, and indeed you will see snowbladers stepping and skating in between carves with no real distinction between the two styles.

The learning process is quite accelerated compared to snowboarding or skiing and quite a bit less physical too!

If the tips don't have much upturn, this makes it more challenging in powder or on crud or other bumps. It's easy to trip over the ends. For deeper powder or 'all-mountain' use it's a good idea to look for wider planks as well.

The 75cm–1m range is best for moguls, trees and jibbing around on the piste. Over a metre is the usual choice for big air or a bit more speed. Of course, the taller and heavier you are, the longer or wider you need, but since the extreme shortness of the blades is the point of the exercise, don't be afraid to experiment with it.

CROSS-COUNTRY SKIING

You won't necessarily see or notice the cross-country skiers (or XC) in the resort. They rarely venture onto the same slopes as the downhill fraternity, instead using specially made tracks and trails on the less steep parts of the mountain, or simply tracks or snow covered roads that exist for other purposes. For this reason, many skiers are unaware that, far from being a minority sport for a few would-be Olympians, cross-country is practised by rather a lot of fitness and snow enthusiasts.

Of course it makes a lot of sense. Cross-country is much cheaper. The equipment costs a fraction of the price of 'alpine' skis, boots and poles, and no special clothing is required beyond that which one might own to go for a walk or a run in questionable weather. And far from being the preserve of super-athletes, cross-country is popular with a wide cross-section of skiers. Despite the fact that it's up there with swimming and rowing as the ultimate all-over workout, it's not uncommon to see elderly people gliding effortlessly along the trail at an age that most non-snow dwellers have long since given up moving around at all!

↑ XC skis don't normally have metal edges like an alpine ski. This means they won't carve a turn, but this isn't normally required.

facilitate glide and with due attention to temperature and snow conditions. The difference with a non-waxless ski is that the middle part is waxed with grip wax.

Depending on the season and the type of snow you'll be skiing, there are different types and temperatures of wax. For good quality snow, hard waxes are colour coded according to optimum snow temperature, and are easy to use. Klister (a soft goo) is suitable for warmer or freeze/thaw conditions, and spray wax is a quick fix when you are out and about.

WAXING CLASSIC SKIS

Classic ski waxing is a black art, but if you ski a lot it may have to be learned. Here are the basic principles.

Apply binder – For coarse snow, you can apply binder wax so that the grip wax won't get rubbed off. Rub the binder wax onto the kick zone, on either side of the groove. Then heat the iron to 40°C/110°F and melt the wax into the ski. After cooling, rub it down with a cork.

Hard wax – Working at room temperature, rub hard grip wax up and down the kick zone. Buff with a cork, apply another coat of wax, and buff again.

KLISTER

Rub the kick zone with a cork. Apply base klister in strips on either side of the groove. Warm and iron it into the ski with a waxing iron at 40°C/110°F. Let it cool and then cork it. Next, apply a universal or snow-specific klister in the same way. Spread it out with a plastic scraper or a cork.

TEST

If you're slipping, the wax is too hard. Remove it with a plastic scraper and then apply a softer wax. If you've got too much grip and snow is sticking to the bottom of your skis, scrape off the soft wax and try a harder one.

Cross-country skis often have a groove down the middle to help them release from the snow. Don't fill the groove up with wax. Make sure it is scraped clean with a suitable tool, as shown right.

CLASSIC STYLE

There are two different ways to cross-country ski, and they require different equipment. The original method, invented not as a sport but simply as a way to travel around in the winter (and hence the origin of skiing – see page 12) is called *classic* or 'kick and glide' skiing. Each ski is slid forward in turn, with the back ski giving a little kick or push to glide forward, further assisted by the opposite pole.

The classic style requires that the ski has some grip on the snow as well as being able to glide forward. This is achieved either by a grippy wax on the underfoot part of the ski, or by scales imprinted onto this area as shown right.

The rationale behind the design of all classic skis is that the middle of the ski will be pressed hard into the snow during the push and kick phase. The scales or grip wax are applied directionally so that they slide forwards easily, but grip when pushed back upon. Applying the grip wax correctly so that this actually happens, though, is another matter.

WAXLESS SKIS

A waxless ski is not, in fact, waxless. The front and back gliding areas of either type of ski should be waxed in the same way as any other ski, to

SPRAY WAX

For if you need a quick fix while you're out on the trail. Spray an even coat from the front to the back of the kick zone. Use one stroke only. Do not cork.

SKATE STYLE

Skate style skis are shorter, less cambered and less sidecut than classic skis. They don't need all the black magic in the mid zone, because the propulsion all comes from the edges. They are therefore waxed the same way as normal alpine skis. Phew!

The boots need to be laterally quite supportive to allow the skating action without injury.

TECHNIQUE

Cross-country skiing is quite easy to 'have a go' at. Classic is more accessible and initially requires no prior skills. Stopping and steering is effected by means of the snowplough. Many cross-country trails feature two grooved 'tracks' made by a special piste machine, which effectively guide your skis around all but the most severe turns. Lift one ski out of the groove if you need to snowplough. The one on the outside of the turn!

Another way to turn, without braking and so popular with racers, is to step the skis alternately around the turn. This works equally well with classic or skate style.

Skate style, clearly, requires that you learn to skate the skis. This is covered elsewhere in the book (page 73). To go fast on the flat in a skate style really requires some training from an instructor.

Cross-country skis can travel uphill, until the gradient is too much for them. Once this occurs, you will need to skate, herringbone or side-step up until it's less steep and normal progress can be resumed. For these techniques see pages 71/73.

POLING TECHNIQUES

The poles are also used to push the skier along, thus engaging the upper body as well as the legs. Instead of gripping the pole grip tightly, the straps are used to deliver the push, since the effort will take place behind the skier.

The timing and rhythm of the poling also varies, depending on slope, ability and pace. You can think of it as different gears.

Single poling – Pushing alternately with each pole as you glide the opposite ski forward is called single poling. It's also called some insulting

⬇ **Cross-country trails are usually groomed into corduroy by a normal "piste-basher", but an additional device also cuts the two parallel tracks for classic skis.**

things like the 'granny skate', the implication being that you are in no hurry, and have no desire to demonstrate any athleticism. Really it's like skiing in low gear.

Double pole each leg – Pushing with both poles on every leg push is a higher gear again, and is sometimes called '1-skate'. Good for going uphill or for accelerating.

Double pole one leg – Also known as offset poling/skating, asymmetric, or '2-skate', this is a way to push hard with both poles, but less frantically. It gives more time to recover the poles and works well at speed. Like a really high gear!

Skating only, sometimes called 'V skate' or 'free skate', is often used going downhill, where you can't add much to your speed with the poles. That's the top gear, perhaps.

Skating is generally faster than classic and has become the more popular style. That said, classic style is the better starting point unless you are already good at skating skis or skates. Each technique exercises different muscles and top athletes train in both disciplines to maintain their overall condition.

BACKCOUNTRY SKIING

Many people like to cross-country ski away from the marked trails, striding off across the countryside wherever the mood takes them. Sometimes called 'breaking trail', this sort of backcountry skiing can be very rewarding as well as quite arduous! Skate style is not usually possible once we leave the groomed trails, and as the snow becomes deeper or steeper, more specialist equipment is required. While normal classic skis suffice for a moderate stroll, many more adventurous skiers choose higher, stiffer boots, and longer skis with metal edges and a bit more float. These backcountry skis effectively bridge the gap between normal XC skis and telemark or touring skis (see pages 130 and 134).

TELEMARKING

It's an odd name, but so many things in sport are named after people or places. And Telemark was the place that made famous a modern (it was modern in the mid-1800s) way of skiing. Now, ironically, it seems at first sight an archaic and unnecessarily difficult way to ski, in its downhill mode at least. But that hasn't stopped it from experiencing a modern resurgence. A Renaissance, if you will...

What is a telemark ski? It's a downhill ski whose binding has a permanently free heel. Cross-country skis have this too, but their boots, bindings and edges are usually too feeble to make carved turns. The telemark ski can travel uphill or cross-country as well, but downhill is usually turned in the distinctive telemark drop-knee style.

Because of this, the skis are usually designed a little differently. A ski designed for touring will have more camber than a downhill-only ski, and an alpine ski will generally be stiffer because an alpine turn powers up the outside ski massively, whereas a tele turn keeps an equal amount of weight on both skis, if at all possible.

Telemarkers generally have to endure a lot of good-natured abuse from alpine skiers. The telemark mantra is:

'Free your heel and free your mind'

But it's often misquoted by downhillers as 'Free your heel, plant your face'! Telemarking is difficult, and that's part of the appeal. The more involved turn protocol means that you have to think ahead a bit more, and the drop-knee position is physically extremely demanding. Once you have it though, it's a beautiful form, and commands a lot of (grudging) respect from most alpine skiers.

Historically, everyone skied in leather walking boots, but now the telemark boot is different from the alpine boot. There is still a flange at the front to engage with the binding, but it's much longer on the tele boot. The toe features a hinge-like bellows that allows the boot to bend at the front to lift the heel. The binding is characterised by a spring-loaded loop that goes around the back of the boot.

The telemark set-up should not be confused with alpine touring kit, which also allows the heel to lift but does so by releasing the whole binding to hinge up from the front. This is then locked down onto the ski for the descent.

→ In common with the other types of touring skis, telemark skis are commonly used in conjunction with 'climbing skins' which allow the wearer to ascend almost straight up quite steep slopes.

TELEMARK TURNS

Many skiers don't notice telemarkers on the slopes, but those who do often stop and stare, 'wowed' by the grace and power of this ancient form. Until the tele skier crashes in a tangled heap, anyway. If you get a chance to have a go at telemarking, though, I do recommend it. Try it somewhere not too steep. A basic green slope is good for starters!

The first thing you'll notice about free-heel bindings is that you can't shunt your whole weight forward to power up the front of the boots. Because the bindings are hinged at the toe, and free at the heel. You'll just fall over forwards.

And this is one reason for the drop-knee telemark turn. It stops you falling forward. Care should be taken, however, when negotiating small drops and jumps or when riding on and off lifts. If in doubt, slide one

↑ **Practising the telemark stance while stationary.**

ski forward and bend the knees. It can save you from an embarrassing wobble. Or face plant!

Some telemarkers adopt a casual turning stance, with the leading knee bent halfway like a recreational alpine skier. This works, but makes it difficult to power up the edges of both skis. The more committed telemarker will drop until the inside knee is nearly on the ski, and next to the boot of the outside ski. The challenge here is to keep roughly the same amount of weight on both skis. The answer is to press down very hard with the toe of the inside (trailing) boot.

Fixed heel skiers who cross to the dark side find it confusing straight away that they are leading with the wrong knee. As do telemarkers who switch to alpine skiing. It is a bit odd that the two disciplines work so … oppositely!

HOW TO MAKE THE TELEMARK TURN

The best thing to do is to practise on the flat. Stand in a natural stance with everything slightly bent as usual, but with the skis close together, less than a handspan if possible. Slide one ski forward and sink down until the shin of the back leg is horizontal-ish. Try to ignore the screams of protest that are probably coming from your quads right now. Concentrate on pressing down with the toe of the back foot so that you feel it's taking as much weight as the foot that has the luxury of being flat.

It should be that in this position, the knee of the back foot is somewhere near the heel of the other one. It's a lot easier on the legs

if you offset them more, but it makes the whole turning unit a) too long, and b) too unstable.

Practise standing up and switching legs a few times, to get the feel for how much you need to shift your feet and how much to drop, and then it's time to take it to the hill!

Set off down the slope on a slight diagonal run and make your first turn back towards the fall line like this. Drop into the telemark position,

TELEMARK TIPS

In alpine skiing, the upper body generally faces the direction of travel most of the time. When telemarking, turn your torso more to face down the fall line. Imagine a torch/flashlight in your navel, and keep it shining down the hill the whole time.

Some people like to learn the tele turn by initiating a snowplough and then adopting the drop knee position once the skis are turning. →

remembering that the forward ski will be on the *outside* of the turn. Now, shunt your hips across to the inside of this turn, concentrating on keeping the pressure on those back toes. If you don't bend the skis equal amounts, they'll head off in different directions! If all goes well, you'll make a long telemark turn.

As you cross the fall line, slowly begin to stand up centred and then down again, switching to the opposite stance, then once you're down shift your hips to the inside again to make the next turn. Once it's all working and you have faith in it, you can squish the timing of all of these things together, but for now, baby steps and one thing at a time.

Touring, ski mountaineering, rando (short for the French word *randonée*), hike-in, backcountry... these are all terms that continue to be used for ways skiers access the areas that are not sanitised by resort measures or served by ski lifts. A step further than in or near resort off-piste, perhaps. It doesn't matter whether you access the pow(der) on foot, by vehicle or helicopter. It all comes under the umbrella of adventure skiing.

Modern ski equipment allows us to access the mountains in a very real way, eschewing the formalities of the resort and trekking wherever the mood takes us. The disadvantage is that there is usually a fairly small percentage of the time spent actually skiing downhill, but for skiers who appreciate adventure travel and getting off the path, adventure skiing is an irresistible draw.

The lack of reliance on ski lifts has a financial advantage, to be sure, but it also means that skiers are not confined by seasonality. If good conditions arise while the resort is closed, you can just load up and go. October freshies or a late spring freeze can be capitalised upon by the more adventurous skier. Just make sure you're waxed up and ready!

It is essential that you have a good level of fitness and skiing ability before you head off into uncharted territory. Adventure skiing's physical nature demands a lot of your body, clothing and ski gear, even in the descent phases. Remember there will be no lifts where you are going. Later we look at altitude and the increased demands on limited oxygen – see page 140. So you need to make sure that you're fit enough to hike through deep snow and up steep slopes unaided. Take some time out to get fit before your trip, and maximise your safety and enjoyment.

It is a good idea to find a qualified local guide. Resorts are relatively safe because they have been organised by the locals to be that way. You can't make a tourist industry out of injuring people. Once you leave the resort you need to know the terrain, and this can only mean enlisting the services of someone who grew up there, so that you don't paint yourself into a corner, so to speak. Winding up on an exposed ridge surrounded by avalanche-prone slopes with nowhere to go but down, for instance. A local can show you the area's secret spots based on your skiing ability, while keeping you safe and getting you home in time for tea and cake. Which is better.

EQUIPMENT

Adventure skiing can take many forms. If you are going up by vehicle or helicopter, you may be on alpine powder or all-mountain skis. Hiking in can be done on foot with skis on your back, but many skiers choose to make ascents or cross deep snow using touring skis. These could be Nordic (telemark) or alpine style. Touring skis are usually lighter than those designed purely for descent, and alpine touring bindings are hinged at the front and designed to release for a telemark-style walking motion. When it's time to descend, the binding clips and locks back down for a fully alpine skiing style.

In addition to the free-heel ski bindings, in order to ascend or make good progress in powder, you need 'skins'. Skins are so called because historically they were made from animal pelts, but these days they are made from nylon with a reusable sticky back. In short, they are fabric strips that fit under the skis and make them work in a similar way to cross-country skis – you can slide your feet forward very easily, but the soles grip firmly on the snow rather than slide backwards. This is achieved because the pile of the fabric (they do look a bit like carpet!) lies in one direction. It's a bit like stroking a shark, or a bird – smooth one way, rough the other. The grip skins deliver is sufficient to march straight up hills of 40° or more, yet still be able to ski down quite gentle slopes without removing them. It is usual to remove them for lengthy descents, though. They make it all feel a bit weird. The skins must be cut narrow enough that they don't cover the edges of the skis, because these need to bite into the snow for safety.

CRAMPONS

When the going gets really tough, and it's not safe just to skin up the mountain, some skiers attach metal spikes or crampons to the skis to give a secure grip on ice or steep slopes. These, clearly, must be retracted or removed for descent.

HELI-SKIING

Unlike other forms of adventure skiing, accessing the best descents using a helicopter doesn't come cheap. But it is surprisingly achievable for many skiers. In areas where commercial heli-skiing is allowed, many operators offer a paying ride to the top for four to twelve skiers. Usually there will also be a guide – the type of slopes that are accessed by helicopter usually come with their own special navigation and safety issues!

Many operations treat the helicopter like a ski lift, picking up and dropping skiers on the best descent slopes for as many runs as can be fitted into the day. In Europe it is more common to use the helicopter to access the summit, for one lift only, leaving the skiers to work their way down to a road or village. This usually means some hiking, because although the trend is generally downhill, this sort of vast terrain is rarely without any dips or bowls.

While it is possible for helicopter passengers to disembark while hovering near to or touching the ground (indeed this is sometimes necessary on very steep terrain), it is more usual for the aircraft to land. This reduces downdraught and turbulence which can cause a whiteout, and makes it a more pleasant experience for everyone involved. The skis are unloaded onto the ground and the passengers crouch in a safe position facing the machine and holding onto their gear until the helicopter has taken off.

It is possible to don your skis in the helicopter and to jump off from one of the skids while the helicopter hovers over a suitably steep slope, but this is in the realm of professional extreme skiers and is more of a stunt than a practical slope access mode.

As with any form of adventurous skiing, heli-skiers must be able to ski whatever type of terrain they encounter, and be able to get down in all possible snow conditions. Avalanche awareness is important, as is all the standard equipment carried by off-piste skiers (see page 145).

CHAPTER SEVEN

SAFETY

MOUNTAIN SAFETY

⬆ **A little powder snow covers the hard ice debris from a previous avalanche at the side of the piste. Very dangerous to stray onto.**

There are a number of basic things you should know about general mountain safety. Above all, you are responsible for your own safety. Ski areas have a lot of facilities, but they aren't Alton Towers. Look out for danger and prevent accidents yourself.

CELLPHONES

Let's face it, cellphones are clever things (where they work) and are one of the most powerful tools for implementing rescue and the logistics that go along with any incident. They can also sometimes tell you where you are! But many people are concerned by the cost of using one in a foreign country, to the point that they switch them off or leave them at home. Instead, think about getting a plan or an additional cheap phone that will actually be useful. It could save your life or someone else's.

Keep your cellphone in an inside pocket where it will be warm, or the battery life may be severely compromised.

Restaurants

ALTITUDE STUFF

Skiers often forget that altitude is a serious matter. In the mountains the air is 'rarified' meaning that there is less oxygen in each breath you take. When you are relaxed and at rest, this may not be a problem, since there is at low level a good deal more oxygen in each breath than you need. But begin to exercise, and your oxygen requirement increases. Then you can start to notice the effects.

Actual altitude sickness (severe headache, nausea, loss of energy) is very rare among skiers. It tends to occur if you ascend from low levels to above 2,400m (8,000ft) rapidly and then stay there for many hours or days. If it does happen, get down lower as soon as possible. This is a typical situation for mountain climbers, but not for skiers. However, there are oxygen issues for skiers at much lower altitudes.

If you live at sea level, and ascend to 1,300m, which is the lowest point of most European resorts, you will already find that everything is a bit more effort, maybe 15% more. Ascend to 2,500m and it's a *lot* more effort. Alcohol also affects you more. It doesn't matter how fit you are. These effects are caused by being at higher altitude than you are used to in your everyday life.

Just take it steady. Don't push yourself to physical extremes based on

what you think you should be able to do at sea level – instead listen to your body and how it feels. And don't drink too much on the mountain – you may be intoxicated on half as much alcohol as down at the bottom.

SUN STUFF

There are often more hours of sunshine on the hill, and UV levels are higher too. Don't take chances with your vision. Make sure you have quality eye protection – good lenses block 100% of UV-A, UV-B and harmful blue light. Check the label. Sunburn is a very real issue too, as well as the famous 'panda tan' caused by tanning the face with goggles on. Choose appropriate sun protection.

STANDING AROUND

The FIS rules of conduct are on page 95. Most of them are just common sense. But there is a tendency for skiers to feel that since they've paid good money for a lift ticket, they somehow have a right to do what they want. Remember that everyone's in the same boat. Don't stand around in places that block other people from getting on with their day. And don't carry on skiing if you can't do it without causing problems.

CROSSED SKIS

If you can, move any incident to the side of the piste for safety. But if someone is hurt, a pair of crossed skis on the uphill side is the accepted way to warn others to take a wide line until the ski patrol arrive with a sled or other rescue vehicle.

SKI PATROL SLED

That's right. If someone is injured on the mountain so that they can't get back down, the ski patrol will ski down with the victim in a sled, unless the injury requires a rescue helicopter. Either way, this isn't free. Insurance should be up to date and cover winter sports medical evacuation, otherwise it's going to get expensive.

⬇ **If there's any sort of feature that the ski patrol fear could cause an incident, like ice or a hole or tree stump, they will try to mark it with crossed poles like this. Off the piste, you're on your own.**

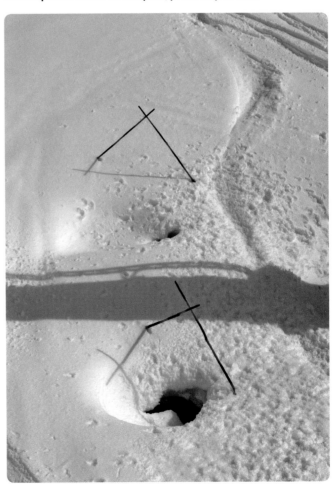

AVALANCHE SAFETY

Avalanches are an ever-present danger in the mountains, but not a threat to the normal resort skier. While they can take place on moderate slopes, the ski patrol and other resort staff are constantly examining the conditions around the resort, and regularly detonate charges to release avalanche-prone snow during the night, to make sure that nothing untoward will happen during the following day's skiing. It's a thankless task and we owe these mountain folk a significant debt of gratitude.

Outside the marked runs of the ski resort, all bets are off. Some of the off-piste is monitored by the ski patrol, if they think an avalanche event might impact on the pistes, but you can't be sure. Sometimes a run will be closed. It's common to see signs warning of dangerous slopes. But you shouldn't take that to mean there is no danger if there isn't a warning! And those who venture into the backcountry are not only at their own risk, but far from rescue if an avalanche happens.

Most avalanche incidents involving skiers or snowboarders happen on slopes with gradients of 25–35°. But that's a bit like saying shark attacks usually happen in less than 2m of water. It's where the people are. Gentle slopes are unlikely to avalanche, but they are usually below steeper slopes that could. And although very steep slopes tend not to hold a lot of snow because it slides off constantly, they still do avalanche, believe me.

FLAGS AND SIGNAGE

In the resort you can benefit from avalanche info updated daily. Here are some of the standard ways the resort will keep you informed.

⬇ **European flag system danger levels 1–2 yellow flag, 3-4 yellow / black chequered flag and 5 black.**

TYPES OF AVALANCHE

Slab avalanche – Under certain conditions a denser and more cohesive layer of snow forms on top of a softer or less cohesive layer. Other factors can also occur, with frozen particles sometimes acting almost like ball bearings or a slip layer between two layers. Anyway the event that occurs is that when triggered by vibration, a large slab of snow breaks away and hurtles downhill. The skier can be carried on top of the slide, but as it disintegrates it typically becomes a tumbling maelstrom of chunks and boulders that overwhelms people and tears them limb from limb before burying them to suffocate.

Sluff or loose snow avalanches – Sluffs are soft, loose surface slides that typically occur in cold weather and good snow conditions, but they are the least dangerous type of avalanche. That said, sluffs can and do injure snow users by carrying them out of control, perhaps over cliffs or into obstacles.

Wet avalanches – These occur when warm temperatures melt the surface layers of the snow and saturate them with water. The water then lubricates the junction where avalanches often occur. Wet avalanches move more slowly than dry, but they are heavy and can still be potentially lethal.

If you are slogging through wet snow up to your ankles while you are on the slope, the snow is wet and prone to avalanche. You can also check if the snow is wet by squeezing it in your hand. Dry snow remains powder when compacted, wet snow drips or becomes ice.

HOW TO AVOID AVALANCHES

Stay on the marked runs in the resort. Simple. If you ask me if you should try skiing off-piste, I'm going to say no. But if you do ski off-piste, here are some things to think about.

The flags and signs in the resort give you some idea of the conditions on the day. The US danger scale is outlined below, whilst in Europe it uses the same 1–5 system with danger levels 1–2 indicated

North American Public Avalanche Danger Scale				
Avalanche danger is determined by the likelihood, size and distribution of avalanches.				
Danger Level		**Travel Advice**	**Likelihood of Avalanches**	**Avalanche Size and Distribution**
5 Extreme	5	Avoid all avalanche terrain.	Natural and human-triggered avalanches certain.	Large to very large avalanches in many areas.
4 High	4	Very dangerous avalanche conditions. Travel in avalanche terrain _not_ recommended.	Natural avalanches likely; human-triggered avalanches very likely.	Large avalanches in many areas; or very large avalanches in specific areas.
3 Considerable	3	Dangerous avalanche conditions. Careful snowpack evaluation, cautious route-finding and conservative decision-making essential.	Natural avalanches possible; human-triggered avalanches likely.	Small avalanches in many areas; or large avalanches in specific areas; or very large avalanches in isolated areas.
2 Moderate	2	Heightened avalanche conditions on specific terrain features. Evaluate snow and terrain carefully; identify features of concern.	Natural avalanches unlikely; human-triggered avalanches possible.	Small avalanches in specific areas; or large avalanches in isolated areas.
1 Low	1	Generally safe avalanche conditions. Watch for unstable snow on isolated terrain features.	Natural and human-triggered avalanches unlikely.	Small avalanches in isolated areas or extreme terrain.
Safe backcountry travel requires training and experience. You control your own risk by choosing where, when and how you travel.				

with a yellow flag, 3–4 with yellow/black chequered flag and 5 with a black flag.

It's important to note that neither in the US nor the European system is there a level zero. Avalanches are always possible. The reports simply give you the likelihood and/or how easily a slide might be triggered.

Level 1: Triggering is possible by groups of skiers on a few very steep extreme slopes. Small natural avalanches (sluffs) are possible.

Level 2: Triggering is possible by groups of skiers, particularly on steep slopes. Large natural avalanches may occur but are not likely.

Level 3: Triggering is possible, even by individual skiers. The bulletin may indicate many slopes that are particularly affected. Medium and occasionally large natural avalanches may occur.

Level 4: Triggering is likely, even with single skiers, on many steep slopes. Frequent medium or large sized avalanches are likely.

Level 5: Spontaneous large natural avalanches are likely, even on moderately steep terrain.

As you can see, an avalanche is more prone to being triggered by a group. So don't all ski into a slope together. For one thing, you are less likely to trigger an event individually. For another, if one person does start a slide, it would be nice if the others were free to search and dig.

TIME

If you are rescued within 15 minutes after being buried, you have a better-than-90% chance of survival. Those who do not survive have usually been killed instantly by the fall. In the next 30 minutes or so, most people succumb to suffocation or other problems. If you are found after 45 minutes you have a 90% chance of being dead (Source: Swiss Avalanche Research Centre, Davos). This is why it is so important to be with a group who are carrying avalanche search and rescue equipment. The resort staff or a rescue helicopter are unlikely to be able to get to you inside 45 minutes.

AVALANCHE EQUIPMENT

It's a testament to skiers' commitment to exploring off-piste that so much equipment is commercially available. If you venture off the beaten track, *everyone* in the group should have the following as a minimum:

Avalanche shovel – A short, break-down shovel than can be used to dig quickly through snow as well as to chip away at heavy ice blocks. Practise using it to dig the car out or make things in the garden.

Avalanche transceiver – The transceiver is always on when strapped in place inside your clothing, and has a long battery life. It can be switched to search mode to find other transceivers. All transceivers are compatible. Practise searching in the garden or around the house.

⬅→ You can buy the whole kit and a special pack to carry it. Some people prefer to carry the gear on the outside of the pack so a colleague can access it.

➜ Always carry a device that can alert the emergency services. A cellphone if there is coverage, or a walkie talkie channel that's monitored. A GPS that can give an exact location will help rescuers, too.

Tip: an avalanche transceiver will detect wifi and cellphone signals at close range (1–3m).

Avalanche probe – A folding fibreglass pole that can be poked down to find a buried skier exactly once their location has been established with transceivers.

Many resorts use the Recco system, which is a search device that the ski patrol or a rescue helicopter can use to search for buried skiers if they are wearing something with the embedded Recco reflector. This is a passive device that is sewn into many items of ski clothing and equipment and requires no batteries or maintenance. Unfortunately, it's only useful if someone is looking for you, and your fellow skiers won't have the search device. So, please carry a transceiver.

Increasing numbers of off-piste skiers are investing in an avalanche airbag system. This is a tough inflatable bag, which is contained in a harness and inflated by a compressed gas cylinder when deployed by the user. If you're caught in an avalanche, you pull the ripcord, and the bag inflates. This helps the skier to stay on or rise to the surface while the snow is still moving. It might be seen as a little like a lifejacket, although it works on a different principle. In snow, unlike water, it is not buoyancy that carries things upwards, but size. Higher volume objects tend to stay at the top while smaller items sink into the mix. The airbag may also help protect you against impacts from hard objects in the avalanche.

RESCUE STRATEGY

Go on a rescue course. There is no substitute in an emergency for having done it all before.

In the event of a slide, try to ski away to the side. You cannot outrun an avalanche. If you are caught, try to stay on the surface as long as possible by deploying your airbag or with a swimming action. You don't get to practise this in advance, much.

If you are buried, try to stay head up and create a space around your face with your arms. Stay calm and wait for sounds of rescue. Saving the limited reserves of oxygen around you is key to longevity now.

If your friend is buried, approach from the side with caution but as quickly as possible, calling the rescue services immediately. Turn transceivers to search and use a regular pattern to cover ground quickly and efficiently. As you get a signal, home in with increasing sensitivity settings until you are right at the victim, then get out the probes to be sure. Digging into the slope horizontally is sometimes easier, but be careful more snow doesn't simply fall into the hole. Clear the head first and then dig out the whole victim while reassuring them. Remember, they may be severely injured. Don't drag them out by the arms.

If you are still waiting for the emergency services, keep the victim warm and hydrated as with any accident or shock situation.

ADVANCED

MOGULS AND BUMPS

Mogul fields are an inevitable part of resort skiing. Some areas of piste can become mogulled in a matter of hours on a busy day. Most steeper ungroomed slopes and easy-to-access off-piste will get there in a few days unless there is fresh snow. The distinctive pattern of regular, domed bumps of hard snow strikes terror into the hearts of beginners, and excitement, perhaps, beats in the chests of the more advanced ones.

Ironically, even some advanced skiers aren't expert at skiing bumps. Many are skilled enough to negotiate the mogul field in control and without falling. But most make the turns that caused this iconic topography in the first place, avoiding the bumps or using them to slow down. The true mogul monster simply bangs straight down the fall line, turning almost but not quite on top of the bumps, and soaking up the attrition with superhuman leg strength. The skis and boots move smoothly up and down like some sort of hydraulic suspension as the skier's upper body barely seems to move at all. It's all very disheartening, or inspiring, depending where you stand on these things.

HOW ARE MOGULS FORMED?

Most skiers would rather go around a bump than over it. We all make turns as we descend the steeper bits of hill, so it doesn't take much mental adjustment to make the turn just before the bump, skidding up against it to lose speed and control slippage. Or to carve around the base of the bump. It is these two practices that make moguls. A small bump gets bigger and bigger as skiers pack more snow up against the high side, and scour snow away from the base. Leaving this distinctive pattern of massive, uniform moguls.

It's interesting to note that moguls don't form on easy bits of slope. They can form on any gradient, from shallow to super-steep, but they always occur where skiers are suddenly out of their comfort zone. This can happen even on the steeper parts of an easy slope, as intermediate skiers come over the brow and slam on the brakes.

DEALING WITH MOGULS

At first, you can't attack the moguls as aggressively as an expert skier would do. As a stepping stone to advanced technique, though, you can begin to embrace the key principle of bump riding, which is to turn near the top of the mogul, not in the trough.

This is where the braquage exercise becomes quite useful. Ride diagonally up the face of the bump, allowing the skis to settle into a sideslip at 90° to the fall line. You should almost come to a stop, with only the foot part of the skis on the snow. Don't wait there, as it's a bit

↑ **The skier slides onto the upper face of the mogul, and with a quick pole plant turns around it.**

precarious, but take this moment when the ends of the ski are free and turn them around the crest of the bump to slide braquage-style down the back facing the opposite way across the hill. Allow yourself a bit of forward motion to adjust position for the next bump, and do the same. Slide up, pivot around the crest, slide down the back. A good place for your pole plant is actually on the next mogul you're going to attack. And that word is the key. Slowly but surely, we're going to start attacking bumps, not avoiding them!

TAKING IT UP A NOTCH

Once you are confident negotiating a mogul field by riding the bumps instead of trying not to, it's possible to dial some of the skidding braquage out of the descent and take a more forward skiing approach. Practise the same thing, skiing diagonally up the face of a mogul, making a turn while the ends of the ski are unweighted, and sliding down the back side slowly converting the slide into forward motion aimed at the next bump. As you go faster, you'll need to be more aware of soaking up the undulations by staying soft at the knees, but strong in intent. Regular use of the ankle flexes mentioned on page 68 will pay dividends too!

As the bumps get bigger you'll need to have a strong physique and especially core fitness, and be looking not at the next bump but the one after. Quick, precise pole plants are important too. Keep your feet closer together than when piste skiing. Really the two skis need to act as one unit, or it's going to get all out of shape!

MOGUL MEISTER

The real mogul expert doesn't slide or brake through the mogul field, but diagonalises every bump as we have been doing while keeping the skis pretty much in the fall line. Up and over the left side of one crest, the right side of the next, with the legs pumping up and down so that the skis stay in contact with the snow but the head and torso don't bounce around. If the timing goes awry or the legs fail, it all goes wrong, so try it for the last few bumps as you ride out of the mogul field, and work back from there!

Powder is often called the Holy Grail of skiing. It's also described quite often as 'skiing nirvana' and places that boast exceptional and regular powder dumps are sometimes called a 'Mecca for skiers'. Religious clichés abound, because skiing powder successfully is a spiritual experience. It really is. Grizzled, seasoned powder hounds can be heard whooping and screaming like little kids as they put first tracks down the fresh. It never gets old...

TOO MUCH LIKE HARD WORK?

Occasional powder skiers often feel that going off-piste is a slog. On the groomed corduroy, they might be confident and on top of their game, but as soon as the going gets deep, they seem to be struggling. This is a shame, because to someone who has good parallel skiing skills, powder isn't difficult. It's just different.

SPEED IS YOUR FRIEND

Powder is a lot more like a fluid than it is a solid surface. You sink in it. If you stop, it's hard to get back on top of it. In this sense, water people like surfers, water-skiers and wakeboarders will get it more easily. Speed is your friend. The more speed you have, the higher you'll ride in the powder and the more effortless your turns will be. It feels like flying!

EVER CHANGING

However, the density of the snow is ever changing, so you need to keep reacting to the forces under the skis with soft but responsive legs and a taut, activated core. To sense this feedback, you must be 'quiet' and listen. Relax, and think only about staying nicely centred over the length of the skis. If you are too far forward on the piste, you get away

with it, maybe oversteering a bit but you look pretty hot. In powder this will be an instantaneous face plant. Equally, if you sit back on the skis you will lose steering control, since only the back half of the tail will be working. Many people settle back immediately on entering powder, thinking to keep the tips up, but this is redundant. What will keep the shovels of the skis up is speed, and speed comes from pointing them down, not up.

HITTING THE WALL

Another reason for a very relaxed and listening stance is that powder is so soft. On the hard pack, if you push too hard on the outside ski when turning, you will end up with a straight leg and that ski will stop helping, leaving all your weight on the inside one. In deep snow the offending ski will simply sink, and you'll get bogged down. You need to tone down the outside ski push that is common in piste skiers, and keep equal pressure on both no matter which way you are pointed. Equally, if you turn too aggressively, the bases will compact the snow into the outside of the turn and you'll feel as if you hit a wall. Some middle ground is required. If you turn smoothly and progressively you can ride around this wall like a skateboarder in a bowl. Trying not to use a 'wall of death' metaphor here. No need.

SUITABLE SKIS

Powder skiing is achievable on any skis, but it's easier on big fat ones. Most modern alpine skis are relatively wide at the ends, and work well. Specialist powder skis are even wider, and often with less sidecut as it isn't really required in the fluid environment of the powder. The latest powder skis are also rockered instead of cambered so that less pressure is required to initiate the turn.

TRANSITIONING FROM PISTE TO POWDER

Or back again, for that matter. When you ride off the hard pack into the soft powder, you don't need to lean back or anything like that. But you do need to maintain a firm core and soft legs, to stop any sudden drag on your legs from unstanding you (see Glossary). When you ski out of the powder onto the piste, it can be vaguely unsettling because your very relaxed, floating stance suddenly turns to vibrating and skittering and the strong urge to engage some edges. I deal with this with a little jump, as if mentally to draw a line. But that's just me...

A good way to practise is to ride down the edge of the piste, following the line of poles. Cruise into the powder, make a turn or two, hop back on the piste, two more turns. This familiarises you quickly with the different ways your skis behave on and off-piste. One little warning though – close to the piste the powder is rarely very deep. You can get away with piste-style riding in shallow powder that's on top of hard pack, because the skis aren't really floating on fine but pressing down into denser snow. So make sure your powder technique is really on song before you decide that you're ready for the back bowl.

FALLING DOWN AND GETTING UP – POWDER VERSION

If you fall in powder, it usually doesn't hurt. But getting up is a battle. The snow is so soft that every time you put a pole or a hand down, it just sinks. You need to pack down the snow with your body to make something firm enough to sort yourself out on. Sometimes you end up making a bit of a platform from which to restart. If your skis have come off, it can be hell to find them again. Search using a pattern and probing with a ski pole or avalanche probe. You all carry those, right? The ski can submarine pretty far under the snow, 'cos the brake levers don't do much in powder.

Know when to give up. You have to get off the mountain in daylight. If you call the ski patrol there's a good chance they have some spare skis and can adjust one to your boot size. If not, you're walking.

There is a thing called a powder ribbon. It looks like a leash, but you don't want a leash because your ski will batter you as you tumble. No, the brightly coloured ribbon is just tied to your ski binding and tucked into your trouser leg. When the ski comes off, there's a good chance the ribbon will be left trailing on the surface.

TREE SKIING

Skiers get their kicks in a number of different ways. Some like the steeps, some the challenge of moguls. For some it's all about the chest deep powder. But there will always be one group of skiers who want to head for the trees.

Trees offer a number of unique opportunities to the skilful skier. The snow quality is completely different in the woods, because as it falls it is filtered by the foliage overhead, and it is not affected in the same way by the sun. So the forest snow feels lighter, fluffier, and fresher than even the newest of powder out in the open. The trees are also a good place to head to when conditions are not ideal – falling snow or low cloud or mist are less of a problem when you have trees all around to give you a sense of perspective and direction. And finally, there's the challenge. You can't simply turn where you want to. There are big, immovable objects littering your path. You *have* to turn.

Of course, the wooded sections are by definition off-piste. When we talk about tree skiing we don't mean a piste that has trees either side of it. We are going properly into the woods, with trees just a few metres apart. No machine can prepare the surface. And by dint of the skill and nerve required to ski there, the woods don't usually get tracked out the way the open mountain does.

But, there's a downside. Tree skiing is potentially dangerous. There are solid objects to hit, and worse still is the threat of the 'tree well'. You see, where the snow has filtered down through the branches of a tree, it will be so fine and light around the base of the tree that it's like a vortex that will suck you in. Turn near a tree, and you're good. Get too close, right under the branches, as can happen all too easily if you mess up, and the tree well drags you into its evil clutches. Unfortunately, what tends to happen is that the skier falls head first into the well, is unable to climb out or right himself, and potentially suffocates as all the denser snow around the tree falls in on top.

For these reasons equipment and communication are key. You must wear a helmet and good quality goggles and scarf or face mask, to guard against impact and whippy little branches. Don't ski alone. Do take your avalanche transceivers, as you always should when skiing off-piste, because if your friend is unconscious or in a tree well, that's the only way they're going to be found. And communicate. It's not always possible to stop or to keep others in sight, so use cellphones or two-way radios or simply shouting and hooting to make sure that the whole team is OK at all times.

Know where you are going and where you will meet. And if you lose track of someone, the ski patrol need to know soon. Not when your mate doesn't show up in the bar.

Don't go through the trees on the last run of the day. Tired or in poor light, this is when accidents happen. At least if they happen on the piste there's some chance of a ride home. In the trees, it'll get dark and you won't be found.

SEEING THE WOOD FOR THE TREES

Most people who find tree skiing intimidating are rattled by the fact that the view in front of them is filled by trees. You can't see through this impenetrable wall! But listen – it isn't a wall of trees. It's just a forest. There's actually a lot more space between the trees than there is timber. So just go around the next obstacle, and the next and the next, until you come out at the bottom. Even if you ski straight down, the chances are you'll only have to make a few minor direction changes to avoid the trees that actually *are* in the way.

Since the snow is by its nature soft powder, you'll want to keep up your speed. But speed and making late decisions about trees doesn't seem like a great combination, so make traverses if necessary, looking downhill until you see past the immediate and get a feel for a long route down. As soon as that route seems to close up, make another traverse and pick another line.

LOOK OUT FOR BUMPS

They aren't moguls. Lumps and bumps in the trees can be a number of things, but usually they are some soft snow over a tree stump or fallen branch. It's quite upsetting as you swish through deep snow to find your skis under a fallen log. So aim to go over, or around lumps, not through them.

BE GOOD AT STOPPING

You'll want to have practised a hockey stop that works in the powder. Sooner or later, you will mess up and it's better to go into some timber, or a tree well, skis rather than head first. Better still is to stop before you get there. Practise it in the open. It could save your life.

DROPS, CLIFFS AND JUMPS

Some people prefer to keep their skis firmly in contact with the snow, but for others, the thrill of skiing drops is unmatched by any other experience. It might seem that only the extremely reckless and foolhardy would deliberately ski off a cliff. And that might actually be true, on this occasion. But a closer inspection of the technique makes it seem at least a little more scientific!

The easiest place to familiarise yourself with flying is in the terrain park. Get used to smaller airs by hitting jumps. They don't have to be kicker ramps – in fact a straight ramp into a tabletop is much easier to deal with.

If you get next to no air (most people approach much too slowly at first), you'll just ski across the tabletop and down the off ramp. If you hit it hard, you'll land on the downslope, which is OK too.

Stay relaxed and ski up the ramp with everything bent and loose. Pay particular attention to the 'O arms' concept (see page 68). Extend your legs as you leave the ramp, but don't forget to relax them again before landing. Now the key thing is to spot the landing. Look at where you think you are going to land, not the horizon, and not your skis.

As you touch down, try to make the whole length of your skis land at once, and try to ensure too that they are pointed exactly down the fall line.

When you are confident landing on the down ramp of an artificial jump, you should have no problem negotiating natural features. Try making jumps over bumps and switchbacks where you know there's a safe and downhill landing. Downslopes are the key. Time to ski off that cliff...

To begin with, though, start small. Choose a little drop, one metre or so. As your experience increases you can gradually build up to bigger drops.

The most important thing is to check out the landing. The landing should be downhill, steep and there should be lots of deep, soft snow. Ideally, inspect it close up to make sure there are no rocks, tree stumps, or equipment left behind by less careful skiers.

CHECKING THE APPROACH

You will need to get as close as you can to the lip to inspect the take-off. You should check whether there's good snow and try to guess how much oomph you will need to reach the steepest or best part of the landing slope. The last thing you need is to hit some random crud on the approach and flop over the edge onto your head. At this point, decide whether you can just drip off the lip or whether you need lots of speed and a bit of a leg pop to clear the obstacles.

Try to mark the spot where you plan to hit the lip of the drop. If possible, also take a mental note of a landmark you can aim for that will give you the right trajectory towards your preferred landing. It is important to know which direction your skis should be pointing vis à vis the fall line because you probably won't be able to see the landing until you are off the lip.

Go far enough up the slope to get enough speed. You don't want to just fall off the edge. A good speed will ensure a better drop and a safer landing.

STAY COMPACT

Once in freefall it is really important to keep a tucked, compact body position with your arms forward and hands together. If you open out or start pedalling or windmilling you will lose control and be in an unsafe landing posture. Not a good combination.

As with the terrain park, *spot the landing*.

Just before hitting the landing you need to extend your legs a bit, ready to absorb the impact, but keep your O-arms thing going on. Your arms and poles can make fine adjustments to your landing angle, and don't forget about ankle flex too. As your skis make contact with the snow drop into a crouch to counter the braking force. Don't lean back per se, but it's better to have a butt bounce or a backslap on the (soft) snow than to end up going into a forward roll, which happens a bit too often. It is also important to land with skis pointing down the fall line. It's tempting to go for a fading, angled landing – somehow it looks as if that would be less impact, but it isn't. It's the downslope that makes this doable. Don't throw that away.

Ski away casually and try to look bored!

VARIOUS TYPES OF SNOW

It's sometimes said that the Inuit have over two hundred words for snow. I don't know if that's true or apocryphal, but one of the interesting things about skiing is that the surface you're playing on is quite variable. It can be different from one day to the next, in exactly the same place.

CORDUROY

On the piste, the prevalent (and ideal) type of snow is freshly groomed corduroy. The resort staff have been out all night turning whatever chopped up mess the day left behind into perfect, flat pistes. The ribbed finish of this snow allows the skis to bite deeper into the surface than they would in smooth, and also gives an element of feedback that is lacking from a polished surface. It's very satisfying to carve down brand new corduroy, and one reason to be on the first lift even if it hasn't snowed overnight.

ICE

In places, usually steeper parts of the piste, the snow will get scraped by skiers and snowboarders sliding down on their edges, and it will become smooth. In certain conditions, depending on temperature and sunlight, it will turn into ice. Pistes can also ice up in high winds. Either way, it's a bit unpleasant. Ski edges don't seem to engage properly, and the bases chatter over any undulations. Directional control is difficult unless you have the strength and carving ability to force the rails to bite. The solution is often to point straight downhill and ride flat through the icy bit, but only if safety and common sense allow.

POWDER

Step off the groomed piste after fresh snowfall, and you're in the snow that many skiers dream about – powder. Fresh powder is like tumbling through clouds. And speaking of falling – if you do, it's generally funny rather than painful. It's not all skiing nirvana though. If the fresh powder is not deep, the snow under it can be big frozen lumps that could cause you to fall or injure you, and any off-piste conditions require that you take adequate avalanche safety precautions. Powder skiing demands some different techniques from the piste.

CRUD

Crud is just old snow that has been chopped up and compacted by countless skiers. Initially, when you cross the tracks of another skier or boarder in fresh powder, it doesn't seem to upset things much. But

⬇ **As you can see from this photo, a thin layer of fresh powder may lie over the tracks from the day before, which could be frozen solid!**

↑ **Skiing in slush is heavy going and soon tires the legs.**

after hundreds or thousands of bases have pounded the snow, it gets a bit denser as well as lumpy. It's technically demanding to ride, throwing the skis around willy-nilly, but it's good for technique – keep soft legs and attack it with gusto.

SLUSH

Slush is what happens when the snow starts to melt in warm conditions. It's very common after about 11am in the springtime. Initially, beginners sometimes quite like slushy snow because it's slower, but the novelty wears off pretty quickly. As you pass from sunlight to shade you can notice big changes in drag coefficient that threaten to trip you up, and slush is always hard work at speed.

SLUFF

Sluff is the loose snow that dislodges easily on steep slopes and slides down like a mini avalanche. It's quite unnerving at first, but it's usually

↓ **Looking up at a sluff fall I have just brought down after me.**

harmless and its very occurrence usually indicates that the slab beneath is fairly stable. If you get caught up in large amounts of falling sluff it can sweep you away, but the snow is unlikely to cause injury – the danger is that you're carried over a drop or into a tree.

CORN SNOW

Spring or 'corn' snow has been warm for a while and is denser and more granular than normal powder snow. Some people quite enjoying skiing it, but it can be heavy and easily turn to slush.

CRUST

Crust occurs when the top few centimetres of powder is warmed by the sun and then freezes again overnight. It looks exactly like nice, fresh snow, but when you ski on it the skis break through the crust and sink into the powder below. If you don't fall, you continue to hurtle along with your boots battering a path through the crust.

DEBRIS

Sometimes you will see large lumps of snow that have been created by an avalanche or piled up by a bulldozer, snowplough or other machine. You can't ski over this type of snow. Don't even think about it!

ARTIFICIAL SNOW

In most resorts these days, there are a variety of snow-making machines designed to supplement the natural snowfall. They spray a fine mist of water into the air, and this freezes into ice crystals before it hits the ground. In years gone by, they used to position these machines all along the pistes to deposit the manufactured snow where it was needed, but the strategy now is to make huge piles of the stuff and then move it around with bulldozer sno-cats. If you see a big, smooth mound of snow like this, it's hard as porcelain and not really rideable. Even after it's been spread out, it's a bit weird and icy. There will usually be warning signs, but be careful!

Y ou can, you know, go skiing without making a trip to the mountains.

The opportunities for doing so fall into two broad categories:

1 Indoor facilities using manufactured snow, just like the artificial snow that supplements the natural stuff in most modern ski resorts.
2 Replacing the actual snow element with an alternative surface. This could be tarmac, or grass, requiring the use of roller skis that bear little or no resemblance to actual skiing. It's a lot more like roller-blading, actually. But far more common is the plastic 'dry ski slope', which uses a combination of plastic surfaces in a way that can be skied on your normal skis.

Snow facilities can now be found in many towns and cities around the world, but none is more impressive (or surprising) than the one in Dubai (United Arab

⬅⬇ Ski Dubai has real snow and proper chairlifts, a mountain lodge, and actual penguins!

Emirates). The city of Dubai may be a lush oasis in the middle of arid desert, but cold is definitely one of the things it isn't. Ski Dubai is the first indoor ski resort in the Middle East and offers an authentic snow setting to enjoy skiing, snowboarding and tobogganing, or just playing in the snow. It's a unique mountain-themed attraction – five runs vary in difficulty, height and gradient, just like an outdoor resort. The longest run is 400m with a drop of around 60m. The ski resort is also the home of twenty penguins!

Dry ski slopes are also found in many parts of the world. The experience is a little different from skiing on actual snow. It's much slower for a given gradient (although it gets quite a lot quicker in the rain), and falling on it can be rather abrasive so tough clothes are recommended, including knee and elbow pads as well as the ubiquitous helmets. The good news is, because it's slow and quite physical to make turns, if you practise on a dry slope everything seems quite effortless when you try the real thing.

The awesome thing about these artificial facilities is that you can go at any time of year. But if you are taking a trip to the mountains to ski, you might want to go in winter! There's a lot of argument about when is the best time to go. Many people simply have to go in the school holidays, and that is inevitably a very busy time on the slopes, with long lines/queues for lifts, lunch and everything else. So if you don't have to go then, lucky you.

Do some research about the regular skiing conditions where you want to go. There are some excellent weather resources and apps available online, too, if you want to make a late decision, or simply to get excited (or worried) about the trip you've already booked. But snow conditions vary. Many people prefer not to go at the beginning of the season, in case there is not yet enough snow. Generally the snow gets deeper as the season goes on, but at some point in the spring it will warm up and the snow will start

⬆ This dry ski slope is in Plymouth, UK, and is a rather impressively large hill. Quite a steep gradient is required to get the same exhilaration as snow.

to diminish, and more importantly it can be heavy and slushy. So, unsurprisingly, the middle of the season is most people's choice. But if you are primarily an on-piste skier, this shouldn't dissuade you from looking at other times, because the quality of snow-making facilities these days means that most resorts simply won't entertain not having any snow!

⬇ In the foreground the distinctive hex pattern of some older slopes, and further away a different style that's more like carpet.

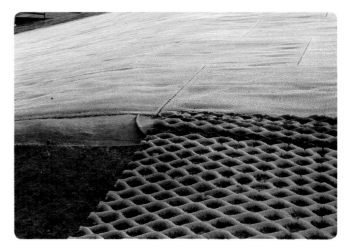

FREESKIING

Freeskiing is a little hard to define. Although primarily associated with tricks and a radical skiing style, in reality it's a skill set, an attitude, and a dress code. And it's very much subject to change. Freeskiing is all about being 'newschool' – pushing the boundaries of skiing beyond what has already been rigidly defined and organised by their instructors or the FIS. It's a youth culture, and perhaps ultimately it just means finding a way to ski that's cooler than whatever your parents are doing.

Currently, freeskiers wear more flamboyant clothes than 'oldschool' skiers, usually characterised by long jackets, hockey jerseys instead of snow skirts, and big trousers. This particular species is usually easy to identify in the wild. Skis are almost invariably twin-tips, and nearly all freeskiers wear helmets. Because they are young, they've grown up wearing them. And they spend much of their time upside down in the air, so it's pretty sensible, really.

This probably happened because snowboarding came along, and was suddenly what all the cool kids were into. Up until the 1990s, skiers had always dressed in a technical and practical manner that was heavily influenced by the athletic wear favoured in competition. Snowboarders were the rebels of the slopes who went the opposite way, wearing baggy clothes for no particular reason except for the fact that skiers didn't. The two camps were clearly separate for decades, but eventually a new group of skiers, who had grown up in a world where snowboarders had always existed, began to adopt some distinctly snowboard dress and behaviour while preferring to remain on skis, albeit skis that had been influenced by snowboard design to be wider, more sidecut than ever before, and turned up at both ends. Like a snowboard.

A big part of the freeski movement is the use of terrain parks and their halfpipes, kicker ramps and rails. When these parks were first installed in ski resorts, it was in an attempt to keep the snowboarders occupied away from the pistes and powder beloved of the skiers. But inevitably, the newschool skiers wanted to play in the parks too, and show the snowboarders what they could do on two planks instead of one. More recently, freeskiers have been found about town, hunting down stairs, rails and other urban objects that they can experiment with.

In truth, I don't like the implication that the skiing world is jealous of snowboarding. Without skiing, snowboarding would never have existed. But we all have influences. And some things that snowboards were better at – like powder riding, and going backwards – were bound to make skiers scratch their heads and try to find ways to incorporate them into their repertoire.

The terms freeski, freestyle and freeride are often used somewhat interchangeably, but there are notable differences. Freeskiing is not the same as freestyle (see page 178) but it incorporates freestyle skiing. It also incorporates adventurous off-piste skiing, and hard charging on the piste. You'll read in the freestyle competition section about all the different freestyle disciplines that a skier can compete in, but the whole ethos of freeride is to invent new ways to do things. And the ethos of organised competition is to annex anything that has become popular, and try to define and regulate it. So freeskiing will always try to be one step ahead. Freeride is a term that was coined by snowboarders, by the way. It means doing whatever you like, on and off piste, mixing up any and every style of riding using only one set of kit. So in that sense to 'freeski' means the same thing. But whereas snowboarders use the word ride, skiers ski, so the freeski movement simply differentiates itself in terminology. As well as everything else.

Technique-wise, freeskiing is invaluable to the sport as a whole, because participants are not constrained by the dogma of previous generations about what constitutes correct posture, style, or anything else. So freeskiers will probably keep inventing new tweaks to their equipment to facilitate something that currently 'isn't done', and finding ever more creative ways to get the best out of the equipment they have. And that, if anything, embodies the nature of the newschool.

⬇ **Twice the fun.**

⬆ **The twin-tip skis that almost all freeskiers use were designed to allow reverse landings and take-offs.**

⬆ **A lot of height.**

Another big air.

Despite normally adhering to a current trend in anti-fashion and of necessity wearing safety equipment, the idea of using fancy dress as a statement comes quite naturally to the freeskier.

EXPEDITION SKIING

For some, an expedition is an exploration of uncharted territory, and few exploratory missions are as arduous as those undertaken across miles of snow and ice. The few who have attempted it have built upon the traditional modes of travel developed by their ancestors, and added modern technology where possible. But mostly it gets drilled down to ice, snow, and skis.

Increasingly, however, it's possible to go on commercial trips – holidays, if you want – to experience the inaccessible interior of extreme environments, using the same sort of equipment and techniques as the cutting edge of exploration employs to this day.

⬆ **Training for an expedition.**

⬆ **A lone woman crosses the ice of Spitsbergen on cross-country skis, dragging her pulk behind her.**

⬇ **Members of the ITACE 2014 South Pole Expedition training with pulks.**

Trekking to the poles is still the preserve of professional explorers, but it is perfectly possible to go somewhere only slightly less Arctic on your vacation, and ski across frozen lakes, pulling your camping equipment behind you in a sled or 'pulk' as they're known.

PULKS

The name comes from the Finnish word *pulkka* and means a low-slung sleigh, used for fun or transport. A pulk can be pulled by dogs or a skier, or in some regions they are pulled by reindeer or horses. The expedition pulk is more usually a plastic or fibreglass tub, which is extremely resilient, not prone to getting stuck in difficult terrain and ideally suited to being loaded up with supplies.

The pulk can be used to carry expedition essentials such as a tent and food, or in Scandinavia it is common to transport a child or old person. In Norway, pulks are normally used by families with small children while cross-country skiing, the children being pulled by the parents, of course. In many places they are pressed into service as toboggans, since the plastic ones are cheap, light and tough.

Larger pulks can be pulled by a number of dogs or persons, and are often used by the military.

KITES

Another way to travel on skis is to be drawn by a kite. The development of kitesurfing in recent years has brought excellent kite technology to snow sports, and four- and five-line kites are both extremely powerful and controllable. The kite is usually attached to a harness rather than taking the strain on the arms, and a 'depower' system is in place so that the skier is not dragged in the event of losing control.

EXTREME SKIING

How does one decide when skiing is extreme? A level of difficulty that is dangerous to the individual is the normally accepted threshold, but since the 1970s skiers have been taking what would be dangerous to a normal individual and adding degrees of gradient and risk that are difficult even to grasp.

The expression *ski extreme* seems first to have been used by French skiers at around that time. European skiers in the 1960s were already beginning to descend slopes that had been considered impossible, assisted by better equipment and new techniques, in particular the jump/hop braquage technique pioneered by Swiss extreme skier Sylvain Saudan.

In the early 1970s the sport took off all around the world, with slopes in excess of 60° being regularly attempted. In 1970 Japanese skier Yuichiro Miura was the first skier to attempt a descent of Mt Everest, although it would not be until 2000 that a successful descent was made all the way from the top to base camp without removing the skis – this was Davo Karničar from Slovenia. As with climbers, there's a movement that seeks to tick off all the 8,000m-plus peaks in the world, of which there are fourteen. Increasingly skiing is also becoming subject to the same 'purity' philosophy as climbing, whereby the use of oxygen is considered cheating.

In order to access many extreme descents it is necessary to hike or climb to the top, which requires the skier to have skills and equipment far above that of the average skier. It is also common to use helicopters to get a skier onto the summit.

For me, the definition of extreme is not so much the gradient or the difficulty of access, but the fact that the skier is entirely on their own. Much like a mountaineer, an extreme skier who makes a mistake on a remote, steep and avalanche-prone face cannot expect anyone to risk their lives to rescue them, or recover the body, and this is a degree of commitment and exposure that is not for the everyday skier, however skilful.

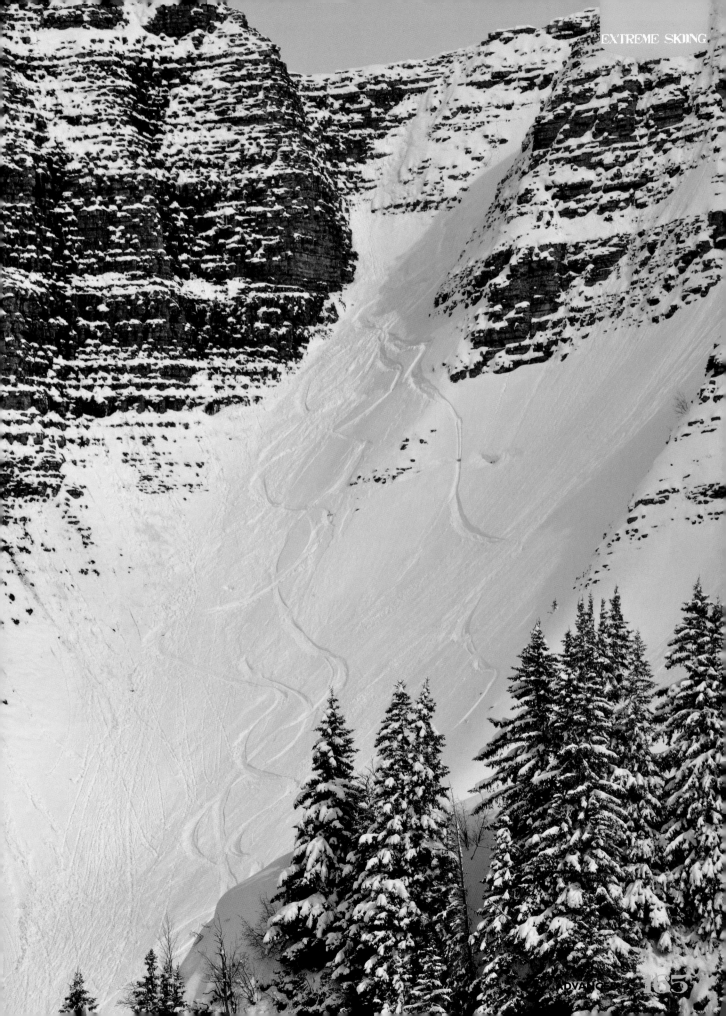

CHAPTER NINE

COMPETITION

PURSUIT OF EXCELLENCE

Maybe you don't need this section of the book. If you just want to go skiing, and have no further ambition than that, then you don't. But, you've picked up a book and read it a bit. I'm guessing there is at least a part of you that is already a little in love with skiing and wants to be more awesome at it. I'm not a competitive skier myself. But I try to bring to the table, so to speak, the same mindset that I used in high-level competition in other sports.

When I first started to compete in outdoor sport, I had no idea about training, or sport psychology, and neither did most of the people around me. What I realised over a period of time was that the more that I was able to mimic the thoughts and actions of the top guys, the more I was able to produce similar results. Even the athletes who just seem ridiculously talented and never train, or worry about their nutrition, still seem to have something to offer if you look at their mental attitude and habits.

In this chapter I mention video a lot. It's entirely my own subjective opinion now, but I don't think it's training to watch countless commercial videos about sport. Sure, it's inspiring – it was seeing the

world's best on the TV screen that motivated me to take up several sports in the first place. And I still watch them sometimes. Or at least the teaser trailer or the edited highlights. But, when you are trying to improve your skills, it's all about achievable goals. So it would be better to spend time watching yourself on video, and people who are better than you but not out of reach. Time and money spent watching the best of the best seems to me flawed in two respects. First, it is time and money that could have been spent on actually enjoying it, or training. Second, a commercial video doesn't show the athletes' everyday performance. It shows their best ever. Which is pretty misleading as a goal. In other sports I have trained a lot of people who said, 'I can do X.' And I would say, 'Can you do it now, when I say go? Or can you just do it sometimes?' And that, fundamentally is the difference. Eventually, even the best work from the best of the best won't be out of reach.

The best way for you to move your skiing forward is to learn how to become an expert at goal-setting and mimicry. If you set achievable yet challenging goals in each of the areas you want to improve, you'll be well on your way. Learn to imitate other great achievers, and you will learn the fast track route to conquering your goals and becoming a champion. Although I can't spend much time on goal-setting here, let me suggest that you be as specific as possible about it. Write your goals down, and use an inspiring photo and a quotation that will help you to feel like a champion every time you see them!

The best way to mimic someone whose performance you admire is to watch them on video. In real life we are always a little bit too slow to pick up on what's important. Take a video camera with you and record everything. Then watch it back, and concentrate not on what the athletes achieved, but what they actually did to make that happen. That's what you need to imitate.

I have outlined a training schedule that helps me. I use it for skiing as well as other sports like kayaking that have different seasons. My year of any given sport is split up into three seasons, the off-season, the pre-season and the in-season.

OFF-SEASON TRAINING

The off-season training begins when the skiing season ends, and is a minimum of two to three months in which I try to recover mentally and physically. Depending on the area in which you live, this period could be longer. During this time, I try to stay active in any way other than skiing. I try to concentrate on activities that will improve my performance the following season. This off-season period should include an aerobic and anaerobic training programme. Bicycling, swimming, weight training, or surfing are all excellent activities that will keep your body developing for the up coming season. In the past I never used to train at the gym, but now I am convinced of the benefits of a weight-training programme that is designed by a professional strength-and-conditioning coach to suit my goals and the season that I'm in. The name of the game is to improve our strength and fitness while not over-taxing the bits on which the ski season has taken a heavy toll.

Although in the off-season I am not skiing, I will still be a skier in my

head. Watching video, reading books, and keeping in touch with the ski world online all help to keep mind and body focused so that when you come to winter again you will bring something more to the table.

PRE-SEASON TRAINING

After several months of not skiing, I am stronger, healthier and more enthusiastic about going again. The main aim during this period is to ramp up the performance from your current ability to the maximum that can reasonably be expected through the in-season. This means concentrating on making sure the basic stuff you can already do is as perfect as it can be, to form the best possible foundation for improving the more difficult skills. These can then be alternated in practice sessions – easy stuff, difficult stuff, with the harder stuff getting the bar raised every time, according to your pre-determined goals. You will need to sit down every couple of weeks and revise your goals. Because you may have set them too high, or too low, and only by comparing progress to goals can you really ever know.

At this point I am still cross-training and training at the gym as well as skills training if I can. Posture, stability, and strength all need to be managed throughout, so that when you arrive at the season proper, you are in optimal condition to ski to the maximum output level up to five times a week.

By training progressively, condition increases at the same rate as the difficulty of your performance. Of course it depends whether you are training for long distance or a 30-second freestyle performance, but whatever it is, work up to it slowly through this period. I find that this is the hardest discipline challenge I face. I love skiing. It's hard for me to do it for just half an hour, at less than maximal output, and then just go home.

When focusing on your training programme, don't forget to concentrate on the basics like warming up and down, and stretching. These are easily overlooked in this build-up phase.

IN-SEASON TRAINING

In a perfect world I would now be skiing five consecutive days a week, under performance conditions and with a focused mindset. Video analysis, if you can get it, continues to allow you to iron out any little kinks in the performance. It takes a lot of willpower to take two full days off, but the recovery time is essential if you aren't to become overtired or even ill.

If the goal is speed, train over race distance. If the goal is a slalom run, do full-length runs. Practise your actual freestyle routine three times back to back and then go and watch it on video, and try again when you are completely recovered. Because that's what happens in a competition. Every discipline is different, but it's very important to practise exactly what you hope to perform. Not twice as much at half the effort, or vice versa!

If you try putting your calendar under this kind of scrutiny, I think you'll be able to accomplish much more than you ever have before. Please be sensible and remember to keep your skiing in perspective though – don't neglect other important areas of your life. Remember, it's just for fun!

ALPINE SKIING COMPETITION

ive disciplines make up the alpine skiing programme today. These are the downhill, slalom, giant slalom, super giant and super combined, all pure racing events. Different courses are prepared for each type of race. At first glance all of the alpine disciplines look quite similar. Lycra-clad athletes race against the clock down a hill marked out with red and blue poles. The differences lie in the proportions of the course and the nature of the gates and turns, and very different skis and techniques are used to get the best performance in each type of race. The downhill event is a race against the clock, usually held on an extremely steep and challenging but groomed piste. Athletes are allowed a practice run to familiarise themselves with the course, which will be at least 1 minute in length, and usually in the region of 1m30s to 2 minutes, with athletes achieving speeds of up to 160km/h (100mph). There are twin-pole flags to indicate the route or limits of the course in places, but the emphasis is on downhill speed and negotiating the terrain, rather than turns. The course will have been designed instead to test skiers with steep, icy descents, off-camber sections, flats and small switchbacks where it is nearly impossible to avoid airtime. For this reason it's considered the most dangerous of alpine disciplines. Increasingly effective safety netting and padding are placed at strategic points to catch crashing skiers, but despite this the inherent risk of the sport is ever present, and there have been a number of deaths and many serious injuries incurred during international-level competitions even quite recently.

Skiers race one at a time at suitable intervals for safety, and have only one actual racing run.

Skis for downhill are different from the other, lower velocity alpine events, being typically longer and straighter than those used in slalom for more stability and speed.

⬇ **Andrej Šporn at the 2010 Winter Olympic downhill, adopting the perfect speed crouch posture. Note the blue lines to mark the course.**

POLES

The poles are made from plastic and are nearly indestructible, necessarily because the skiers hit them at speeds of up to 130km/h (80mph). They are inserted into the hard snow with an ice screw drilled with a portable power tool. Slalom poles have a robust rubber hinge at the bottom, similar to that found at the base of a sailboard mast. Or on a vehicle engine mounting.

⬇ **Slalom chinguard.**

⬇ **Slalom shin pads.**

The word slalom, now used in many different sports throughout the world, actually comes from skiing, and even more originally, from the Norwegian dialect of the Morgedal region, home of so many things skiing related. The word 'slalåm' means 'gently sloping track' and was used in Telemark for ski trails without severe obstacles, which were considered suitable for practising on.

SLALOM COMPETITION

In modern slalom, the athletes race against the clock down a course made up of 'gates' – each gate is a pair of red or blue poles and the skier must pass between them – which are in quick succession but spaced and positioned with considerable variety so that the athlete cannot find a rhythm or pattern. Some portions of the course, for instance, will have the skier hitting more than one gate per second. Others will be further apart, but rarely more than one or two seconds. The poles are mounted on rubber hinges so that the skier can knock them out of the way with the body. With correct technique the pole is struck with the shins and the outside hand. The skier wears armoured shin guards and gloves as well as a helmet with a chin guard, as striking 50 of these hard plastic poles at high speed in less than a minute threatens considerable attrition!

Beginners and children sometimes practise with mini gates that

only come up to knee height, to develop the technique without the battering!

The rules dictate that the tips of the skis and the skier's feet must pass through every gate. Missing a gate would mean having to go back and that's just not practical time-wise, so 100% accuracy is required.

The course will consist of around 50–60 gates, over a distance of about 200m.

To the casual observer the course is extremely confusing. Some gates are wide so that one pole seems pointlessly far outside the course, some are narrow, and many are set vertically so that it's

⬆ **Without a skier on the course, it's extremely difficult to fathom the intended route, even though previous skiers' tracks give some indication.**

hard to see where they are. Course designers construct each course uniquely and individually, and go to some trouble to make them tricky to read at speed as well as physically and technically challenging.

Athletes must ski two different runs in the course of a competition, and their final time is aggregated.

GIANT SLALOM

In the giant slalom, sometimes designated GS, the course is much larger and the turns are less fast and furious, but it is still very much a turns event rather than a 'race with corners'. The regulations allow for a 50% wider course, and the number of direction changes is dictated by the rules as a function of vertical drop in metres. Under current legislation, a 300m course would have 33 to 45 direction changes. So you can see straight away that being longer, wider and with fewer turns than a typical slalom, giant is going to have a very different feel. The turns are usually marked with the twin-pole flags associated with downhill racing, too, and without the necessity to understand the direction and nature of the gates.

It's a lot easier to see what the skier is meant to be doing!

Giant slalom skis are longer than slalom skis but shorter than those used for downhill or super-G. Ski lengths and other parameters are dictated by ever-evolving regulations, but one of the more interesting areas is the sidecut of the skis. Since the adoption of more side curvature in most types of skis in the 21st century, athletes have been able to make tighter turns, and interestingly the number of knee injuries has tended to reduce. The FIS have, however, included a minimum sidecut radius as a limit to performance. At the time of writing, this radius had recently been increased to 35m for giant.

This rule I often misunderstood.

The sidecut radius is a dimension of the ski, not the minimum radius turn it can make in the snow. Clearly, by edging the ski at more extreme angles and attacking the turn to bend the ski more, it can turn much more tightly than that even without skidding. In fact, when the regulation minimum radius was 27m for men and 23m for women, multi-championship winning skiers Ted Ligerty and Lindsey Vonn (both US racers) opted to use 29m and 27m respectively. The theory is that with sufficient technique and power, an athlete can actually gain a performance advantage from a less sidecut ski. Ligerty famously opposed the latest increase in radius, but then went on to win on the new skis anyway, being one of the few skiers who could get the best out of them. He described attacking early in the turn as a risky strategy requiring more strength and balance.

Again, two runs are made and the times are added together.

SUPER-G

As the name suggests, Super-G is an even bigger version of giant slalom. There are still widely spaced turn markers, but the trajectory is more down the fall line like slalom and the speeds are comparable with downhill racing. In fact, the Super-G event is usually held on the lower part of the downhill run. The dimensions for equipment are commensurately larger, too, with the minimum sidecut radius for Super-G currently at 45m. The other notable difference is that there is only one run for each skier in a super-G competition.

SUPER OR ALPINE COMBINATION

The super combination is as the name implies a combined event, in the same way as the Nordic combined. It involves a pair of slalom runs and a downhill (or a Super-G) run, with the different disciplines being held on separate days. There is also a super combined version, with only one slalom run and a shorter downhill race. This was introduced to balance out the advantage of slalom specialists in the event. The scoring is simply the aggregate of all the runs for each skier.

MORE...

With the exception of the downhill race, skiers do not get to practise the run. They get a time window (usually an hour) to inspect the course, during which they will be visualising their line and mentally running through their body language. Despite this, there is often an advantage to going first and having clean, un-cut-up snow to race on.

Ski poles for racing are often bent into a recurve so as to fit around the body, and usually have aerodynamic, cone-shaped baskets. In all alpine disciplines, athletes wear skin-tight Lycra to minimise drag, and helmets are mandatory.

⬆ **Some events are held with two racers at a time on parallel courses.**

⬅ **These skiers are preparing the course before an event by sideslipping down it, smoothing out the snow. It also gives them the chance to see the course close up, but they don't get to practise it in anger.**

➡ **Sometimes course designers provide a blue line painted on the snow to show the correct route down the course. Without this it can be very hard to set the approach to the next gate.**

⬇ **Racing skis sometimes, but not always, feature a hole in the tips that is intended to reduce air (and snow) resistance at speed.**

SKI JUMPING

The competitive sport of ski jumping has been with us since the early 1800s. With its beginnings in Norwegian daredevils jumping over rooftops, it rapidly evolved into a formal discipline with standardised jump hills and a carefully designed landing area.

Jumping is a Nordic discipline, in that the skis have free heel bindings, allowing an arrow-like aerodynamic posture during flight. Traditionally, ski jumpers have landed in a telemark stance because of this design, but more recently the bindings have begun to incorporate a safety device to stop the boots lifting too far from the skis, and this now facilitates a more alpine style of posture on landing. Poles are not used in competitive ski jumping.

The first recorded public competition was held at Trysil, Norway, in 1862. At this event, judges awarded points for style ('elegance and smoothness'), and participants were required to complete three jumps without falling. The first known female ski jumper participated at this same Trysil competition in the following year, and Norway's Sondre Norheim jumped 30 metres (99ft).

In 1866, the first skiing event held in Christiania was a combined cross-country, slalom and jumping competition, and attracted an audience of some 2,000 people. Sondre Norheim won his first competition in Christiania in 1868.

Until 1886 jumping and cross-country was a single integrated competition. After that the Norwegians began to hold the two events separately, but to combine the scores to give an overall winner. This dual discipline still exists to this day, and is called the 'Nordic combined' – to distinguish ski jumping competition only from Nordic combined, it is still referred to in Norwegian as 'spesielt hopprenn' ('ski jumping only')!

MORE INTERESTING DATES

Ski jumping has been part of the Winter Olympics since the first Games in Chamonix Mont-Blanc in 1924.

In 1929, Norwegian instructors travelled to Sapporo to train the Japanese in ski jumping, and the sport remains extremely popular in Japan to this day.

The Large Hill competition was first included on the Olympic programme for the 1964 Olympic Games in Innsbruck.

WOMEN'S JUMPING

Women have had a chequered history in ski jumping. While there was clearly no discrimination in Norway in the early days, women were later excluded from jumping competitions and it was not until 2009

⬇ **Ski jumper in flight.**

that they first competed in the World Championships. A proposal to include the women's event in the 2010 Winter Olympics in Vancouver was rejected amidst much legal wrangling, and it was finally accepted for the Sochi Olympics in 2014.

Some experts also believe female ski jumpers require a longer approach than their male colleagues to make up for their lighter weight.

HILL DESIGN

Ski jumps look terrifyingly high – if you ever get the chance, go and stand on one. It's alarming. However, though the hill itself is huge, the jump is only a few meters higher than the landing hill. The pre-jump slope has a gradient of 36–38°, which then reduces smoothly so that at the take-off it typically has an angle 7–12° *downhill*.

The landing hill is fashioned in a curved shape to mirror the expected flight, so that the skier is never too far from the ground, maybe 6m (20ft). The steepest point of the hill is called the construction point, critical point or K-point.

The hill size point is the line across the hill where the curve of the landing slope gradient becomes less than 32°.

The hill size is the length from the take-off in a straight line to the knoll and then along the landing slope to the hill size point. After the hill size point the gradient will reduce until level and then maybe a bit uphill, to help the jumper slow down.

Ski jumping is about distance, using the body and skis to help generate lift as you travel through the air, just as an aircraft wing does. Being better at doing this makes for a further flight. The points are currently awarded as follows. Sixty points are awarded for reaching the K distance. After that, points are typically added at a rate of two points per additional metre (this can vary with hill size though). On top of that, three judges have an allocation of up to 20 points each to allow for 'form'. They will reduce this if there is bad form, a wobble or bad landing for instance. So the most an athlete can score on top of the distance points is 60, but it might be less if it's a messy jump. Athletes normally make two jumps, and the scores are aggregated.

There's also a thing called the 'fall line'. This is nothing to do with the fall line we skiers are all familiar with. It's a line on the hill that the skiers must get past without touching the ground with anything other than the skis, if the jump is to be counted.

Jumping skis may be no longer than 146% of the total height of the competitor.

TYPES OF EVENT

Small hill competitions are typically around 90m (300ft). This is sometimes referred to as K90 or HS90 (K-point or Hill Size).

The 'normal hill' competition uses a hill size of 105m (345ft) – HS105.

The large hill is, predictably, even bigger at HS140, so the competitors typically fly for at least 140m!

There is often a team event, too. Teams consist of four people, and the team with the highest total score for all jumps is declared the winner.

Ski flying is a special event with a hill size in excess of 185m. The Ski Flying World Record of 246.5m (809ft) is held by Johan Remen Evensen, and was set in Vikersundbakken, Norway in February 2011.

Amateur and junior competitions are held on the smaller hills.

↓ **Small, normal and large.**

FREESTYLE SKIING

MOGULS – AERIALS – HALFPIPE – SLOPESTYLE – SKI CROSS

Freestyle competition first appeared as a demonstration event in the Calgary 1988 Winter Olympics. Mogul skiing was added as a full medal event for the 1992 Winter Games in Albertville. The aerials event was introduced for the 1994 Winter Olympics, Lillehammer, and ski cross had its debut at the 2010 Games at Vancouver. Finally, ski halfpipe and slopestyle, events previously more often associated with snowboarding, came to the Winter Olympics for the Sochi Games in 2014.

The **mogul** event is, as it sounds, a descent down a mogul field, but athletes are required to deliver two jumps/aerial tricks on the way down. Points are allocated for the technical quality of the mogul riding and the style and difficulty of the jumps, and then points are added on for speed based on a formula. So it is against the clock, as well as being a freestyle discipline. Actually this sport feels like a bridge between classic alpine athleticism and freestyle, rather than a pure freestyle event. Mogul skis for men are typically around 180cm long, and women's skis are 170cm.

CONTRASTING COLOURS

In moguls, the colour of the skier's knee pads often contrasts with that of the ski suit in order to draw the judges' attention to the skier's expertise.

The **aerials** event is jump tricks. The athletes hit a large kicker ramp, perform multiple flips and rotations in the air, and land on a downslope. They are judged for form on take-off, technical difficulty and landing. It's more analogous to Olympic diving than anything else, such is the number of tricks linked in the air. Again, it's a much more formal sport than we normally associate with freestyle but perhaps more in line with the athleticism of the alpine disciplines. The aerials event uses a standard length of ski for everyone, at 160cm.

The **ski cross** event is a race down a course perhaps 1,000m long, negotiating corners as well as obstacles like jumps on the way. It can be individual athletes or up to four at a time on the course, which makes for some carnage and is very exciting for spectators, since unlike parallel racing disciplines, the athletes are vying with each other for the best line and can often interfere or collide. Ski cross uses the same type of skis as Super G.

In the **Ski halfpipe**, athletes perform in a halfpipe slope on freestyle skis, riding up each side of the pipe to perform aerial tricks like somersaults, flips, grabs and spins. It's all about carrying enough momentum to get big air each time, so it's a trade-off between riding across the pipe and riding down it for speed.

⬆ There are halfpipes like this in most terrain parks, but high-level competitions and Olympic venues have a superpipe, which has much higher sides and is quite dangerous and intimidating!

Ski slopestyle. Athletes perform on a slope with a downhill sequence of terrain park obstacles like rails, kicker ramps and other jumps. The technical characteristics of the course are dictated by FIS rules, but the skier chooses their own routine of tricks to impress the judges with smoothness and technical ability.

CROSS-COUNTRY SKIING COMPETITION

Cross-country, arguably the original competitive skiing discipline, has been contested at the Winter Olympics since the first Games, held in 1924 in Chamonix Mont-Blanc. It's one of the Nordic (free heel) disciplines, like jumping, and as such is part of the Nordic combined competition as well as a sport in its own right.

There are separate races for classic and free-skate technique, and a variety of different distances and formats for each. Individual events see athletes set off at intervals, whereas the mass start event can have 60 or more athletes jostling on the start line.

The distances vary enormously, with sprint events of only 1.5km right up to 50km+ races. It seems that the introduction of that shortest distance in 2002 has contributed to a big increase in the audience popularity of cross-country competition. Longer events now being held with multiple laps through a stadium are also much better for both the crowd and for the television audience.

The FIS official Olympic distances are currently as follows: Women compete in the sprint (1.5km), team sprint, 10km individual start, 15km pursuit, 30km mass start and the 4×5km relay. Men

Biathlete

compete in the sprint, team sprint, 15km individual start, 30km pursuit, 50km mass start and the 4×10km relay.

Outside of the Olympic racing structure, there are various races around the world in the region of 100km, and the Canadian Ski Marathon, which is a tour rather than a race per se, has its longest distance challenge at a staggering 160km.

The skiathlon is one of the most exciting cross-country events. The athletes race the first half using classic technique, and then switch to free (skating) technique for the rest of the distance. The clock keeps running while the skiers change skis, so it's a bit like a pit stop. The first skier to cross the finish line wins. Men ski a total distance of 30km, while women race over 15km. The competition circuit is usually designed so that skiers do several laps for a better spectator experience. There are also relay events for teams of four.

BIATHLON

Biathlon is not two separate disciplines, but a race in which cross-country skiers carry a rifle on their back, and stop at intervals to shoot targets. This is of course immensely challenging, not just because of the extra weight of the weapon but also the difficulty of making a steady aim when exhausted after racing over long distances.

The athletes ski around a cross-country trail system, and the total distance is punctuated by either two or four shooting rounds. Half are in the prone position, the other half standing up. Depending on the shooting performance, extra distance or time is added to the contestant's total running distance/time. It's a race, so the skier with the quickest total time wins.

For each shooting round, the biathlete must hit five targets. Each missed target must be dealt with in one of the following ways, depending on the competition format:

1 By skiing around an extra 150-metre (500ft) loop. This would typically take 20–30 seconds for a top-level biathlete.

2 By having a time penalty added, usually one minute.

3 By having to take another shot using an extra cartridge placed at the shooting range to finish off the target. Only three such 'extras' are available for each race, and a penalty loop must be made for each of the targets still left standing.

The racers are allowed to use any skiing technique, which means that the predominantly skating free technique is used, that being the fastest.

The different events in biathlon are as follows:

■ **Individual** – 20km for men and 15km for women, with four shooting rounds and 20 targets in total. Skiers set off at intervals, usually 30 seconds.

■ **Sprint** – 10km for men and 7.5km for women, with two shooting rounds. Again, athletes start at intervals.

■ **Pursuit** – starting at intervals determined from a previous race, but the first to cross the finish line is the winner.

■ **Mass start** – all athletes start at the same time and the first to cross the line wins.

There are also relay events which are commonly held in teams of four.

The rifle, which must be carried throughout, weighs 3.5kg (8lbs) excluding ammunition, and is a bolt-action .22 rimfire weapon.

FREERIDE COMPETITION

By definition, the concept of freeride is diametrically opposed to that of competition. Some skiers choose not to enter contests because of this clash of interests, and many more simply would prefer not to be judged.

For some riders, however, freeride and competition do go together. I suppose it's an extension of a non-competitive style, but wanting your skiing performance to be appreciated in the bar at the end of the day. It's not a big leap from there to want to compare yourself to other skiers from time to time and have someone decide who put on the best show.

That's why freeride contests exist, with a formal structure, and judges.

But what criteria are they judging upon? Well, it's usually subjective. Systems have been tried that apply points for different things, whether speed, tricks, whether it was a brave line... but in the end it's proved better to have experienced judges watch a run down the mountain and just rate it out of ten. It's up to the skiers to try to find the coolest line or most radical line down the hill.

Competitors go one at a time, usually from the very top of a mountain in very steep terrain featuring deep powder, drops and ridges. Any route is OK, if it's rideable, and designed to impress the judges. Often skiers fall, but on such steep slopes they usually regain their feet and keep riding, though they may be penalised for the tumble.

The judges watch each descent, usually from a completely different hill using binoculars, a TV screen or their naked eyes to judge. A judge has to consider at all times how fast, how radical, how in control a rider is compared to another. How difficult, steep, or exposed was the line and in what snow conditions the action is happening. There will usually be a number of judges and a head judge who considers the scores to determine whether they are too varied or merit further discussion.

When it comes to freeriding, there are different types of terrain and different ways to express oneself upon it. The goal of the judging system is to allow any style of skiing to win on any given day. Whether a rider's speciality is steep terrain, big air, technical tricks or outright speed, any style should be able to win if on that day, the rider simply showed the most impressive run playing to his own strengths.

As the World Freeride Tour organisers put it: 'Riders shouldn't have to adapt their riding to a system; the system should adapt to the riding.'

So how can there be a judging system that is both fair and still in keeping with the spirit of freeride?

Freeride competition has the same dilemma as other freestyle sports such as surfing, skateboarding or freestyle skiing/snowboarding. These respective sports have all gone through their own developmental processes and it is interesting to note that they all ended up with similar judging systems. Systems with overall impression scores, judged mostly by former competitors respected by the new competing generation. Judging based on subjective emotional response rather than on soulless, mechanical rules.

Inevitably, all the riders will be scored in relation to the first rider

down. In order to give a score to the first rider that leaves room to move, judges must prepare themselves accordingly.

They will check the face and analyse possible lines, think about no-fall zones and the best jumps, and imagine what could be a very hard or safe line on the mountain.

They will garner intelligence about snow conditions to know if, and where, there will be heavy sluff, perfect powder, crusty snow, or ice. To do this they will send experienced freeriders to recce the various routes and give a feel in advance for the sort of runs that might occur, as well as getting the information back about the mountain.

THE NO-FALL ZONE

Judges do have to consider where falls happen. The contest will usually have pre-discussed no-fall zones on the basis of safety. If a rider makes a mistake in a place where he is putting his life at risk because of extreme exposure, he will be penalised. Skiers should understand that they are not to take unnecessary risks in highly dangerous places. Obviously, the same backslap or 'butt check' will not be treated as seriously after a giant drop as it would be if it was a rookie error. The same applies to the form landing a flip or spin compared to a simple jump.

Things the judges will look for and think about (without creating a list of criteria too much!):

- Is the line original, easy or difficult? Does it have big jumps? Was it well thought out or was the skier looking for a way down?
- Is the rider going fast for where he or she is on the mountain? Hesitating or nailing it?
- Is the skier in control at all times? In control in the air and on landing? Did he/she manage to carve in steep narrow places or just slide down?

GLOSSARY

AFD Anti-Friction Device, usually referring to a bit of the ski binding that aids boot release in a fall.

Braquage Turning without edging, using body language and sideslipping technique, as an exercise or to control speed.

Bunny Bunny slope means the children's learning area. Ski bunny is a sexist and mildly derogatory reference to an attractive woman who skis.

Cat Short for Caterpillar. As in the brand of machinery. Not an animal.

Cat Track A narrow track or piste just wide enough for a piste basher.

Centre of gravity/mass (CoG/CoM) The point from which the weight of a body or system may be considered to act. In uniform gravity, the centre of gravity is the same as the centre of mass.

Centrifugal This is a force that acts on a body moving in an arc, directed from the centre of mass towards the outside of its locus.

Centripetal This is a force that acts on a body moving in an arc, directed from the centre of mass towards the inside of its locus.

Christie Antique name for a turn coined by Brits in the 1920s. Short for Christiania.

Corduroy The unique combed pattern of extremely unfashionable trousers. And pistes.

Core (of body) A fashionable term for the collection of muscles inside the lower torso that primarily control posture.

Core (of ski) The magic engineering bit inside your ski that gives it the right amount of rigidity and structural integrity. Often made of wood.

Cross-country Type of skiing that is propelled by the skier, not gravity.

Detune Making the base of the ski slightly rounded in section (think boat shaped) to aid edge transitions.

Fall line The line of steepest gradient down a hill.

Groomed A piste that has been flattened and combed.

Groomer A name for the piste basher or the piste thus bashed.

Handiski A European term for sit ski.

Hard pack Snow that has been pressed down and is now hard.

Herringbone Used to describe stepping up the hill in a skate stance rather than sideways, leaving a fishbone-like pattern of marks in the snow.

Inside ski The ski on the inside of the turn or intended turn.

Isometric Muscle contraction or effort with strain but no motion.

Isotonic Muscle contraction with motion but low strain.

Kicker A type of ramp with a concave curvature to add jumper rotation as well as height.

Klister A type of soft wax used for the kick zone of cross-country skis.

Lat (latissimus dorsii) Large muscle in the sides of the torso that hurts after excessive flailing.

Nursery slope Beginner's slope – see bunny slope.

Outside ski The ski on the outside of a turn or intended turn.

Parallel turn A carved turn with skis parallel. Used to be the pinnacle of skiing skill until the 1980s.

Piste A marked trail or run for skiing on.

Piste-basher The tracked vehicle that flattens and combs the piste while you are asleep.

Plyometric Explosive movement or exercise – jump training.

Pronation Feet lean inwards (can be caused by being knock-kneed).

Quads Short for quadriceps, the biggest muscle in your thigh, and the most important for skiing.

Rail 1. The edge of the ski. 2. A feature of the terrain park.

Rando/randoneé French word for ski touring/walking.

Recco Passive rescue reflector that is built into many forms of clothing and equipment.

Redirect Point the skis somewhere new.

Rep, reps Short for repetition, this means repeating an exercise a certain number of times: 'Do ten reps'. It also means a type of person who is ostensibly employed by a tour operator to make sure you have a good time, but actually to help you spend money, and mostly just installs hangovers.

Shovel A spade carried by off-piste skiers for avalanche rescue, and building jumps.

Sit ski A type of skiing where the rider sits on a seat with skis underneath.

Skate To propel the skis with a skating action.

Skins Magic carpets attached to the bottom of skis to facilitate uphill travel.

Slarve Sliding carve. Another way to make a turn.

Sluff Loose snow that can be dislodged by the skier. A loose snow avalanche.

Sno-scoot A snow toy a bit like a scooter.

Snowplough 1. A thing attached to the front of a vehicle for clearing the roads. 2. A type of turn with the skis in a wedge shape reminiscent of the days when snowploughs were…

Snowproof Something which will prevent the ingress of snow, but isn't necessarily waterproof. A lot of skiwear is snowproof but not suited to rain or extreme weather, because in this way it can breathe better, which is more comfortable.

Soft legs Keeping the legs flexed enough to absorb bumps.

Spin out Loss of grip at the back of the skis causing a spin.

Steeps Slopes that are challengingly steep.

Stem The skinny bit of a wine glass. And an old-fashioned name for making a wedge shape (either way) with the skis.

Stivot Steering pivot – a type of sudden turn.

Supination Feet lean outwards (can mean bow-legged).

Table-top A type of jump with an up, a flat top and a down bit.

Terrain park An area of jumps, halfpipes and pseudo-urban features for freestylers to play on.

Transceiver An avalanche rescue device that is strapped to the body. It sends a signal all the time, and can be switched to search mode to receive signals from others.

Traversing Travelling across the hill with a minimum of loss of height.

Tricep Large muscle in the back of the arms that hurts after excessive poling.

Unstanding A word I made up. If we were talking about equestrianism, one might say 'unseated'. But we aren't, are we?

Veloski A kind of snow toy that is ridden like a bike.

Waterproof Meaning that it will keep water out in rain, wet snow, or if dunked in a puddle.

Wedge A pointy-shaped thing. In skiing it usually means tips of the skis together (as in snowplough) – wedge turn.

XC Stands for cross-country, for reasons which I would hope are obvious.

BIBLIOGRAPHY AND FURTHER READING

I have referenced the following sites for medical and safety info:

British Medical Journal 2005 citation BMJ 2005;330:281
The New York Times http://www.nytimes.com/2014/01/01/sports/on-slopes-rise-in-helmet-use-but-no-decline-in-brain-injuries.html
Swiss Avalanche Research Centre http://www.slf.ch/english_EN

Also referenced page 12:
Beschreibung von dem unter schwedischer Krone gehörigen Lappland
Hergstrom, P (1748). . Leipzig: von Rother.

These books have been invaluable to me in understanding the learning process and the principles of performance skiing:

Go Ski Warren Smith, ISBN-13 978-1-40531-617-0
The All-Mountain Skier R. Mark Elling, ISBN-13 978-0-07-140841-7
Ultimate Skiing Ron LeMaster, ISBN-13 978-0-7360-7959-4
Really Cool Telemark Tips Allen O'Bannon & Mike Clelland, ISBN 978-0-7267-4586-9

Also interesting are:

Skiing Henry Beard & Roy McKie, ISBN 0-7611-2820-4
Back On The Piste Barry Waters, ISBN 0-356-12565-3
Skiing Fred Foxon, ISBN 1-85223-571-3

USEFUL ADDRESSES

UK / Ireland
skiclub.co.uk
ifyouski.com
snowandrock.com

US / Canada
freeskiers.org
ski.com
skicanada.org

AUS / NZ
ski.com.au
snow.co.nz
freeskier.co.nz

ACKNOWLEDGEMENTS

A book like this relies heavily on its contributors and sponsors, without whom I would have been scratching around looking for skis and kit in friends' garages, and frankly it wouldn't have looked half as good! I have included a little about each one of them here.

I would also like to mention my sincere thanks to all of the photographers, whose names appear opposite and are annotated with the locations of their contributions.

Furthermore, I must thank models Will Badenoch, Nikki Ball, Joanne Davies, Elsa Devaux, Rebecca Dutton, Camilla Evans, Ron Fischer, Joshua Gosling, Kai Mitchell, Alan Staple, Stewart Stirling, Leanne Ward, Maximilian Winter, Zöe Magdalena Winter, who provided their time, skills and infinite patience to helping shoot the technique stuff. It's one thing being able to ski, and quite another to look good doing it on demand. A number of unnamed skiers are also included in the photos, and I hope they too like what they see.

Thanks also to:

- Tord Nilson from Amer Sports PR for help with Atomic photos and equipment.
- Wink Lorch of Chalet Balaena for invaluable help, support, props, and wine!
- Will and Sarah Badenoch of Plymouth Performance Gym.

I extend my gratitude to all of the above, and anyone I may have forgotten, and hope that they like the book that their efforts made possible!

VEST-TELEMARK MUSEUM

The starting point for any visit to Morgedal, this is a striking building which houses a multimedia journey through skiing's history with special attention paid to the skiing revolution which developed out from Morgedal in the 1850's. You can explore the museum on your own but a guide is highly recommended. Jazz lovers flock to New Orleans, Elvis fans congregate in Memphis, ski enthusiasts travel to the little mountain valley of Morgedal. What do they all have in common? The search for the origin... Maybe it is time you took the skiers pilgrimage to Morgedal - no flashy chairlifts, ritzy bars or designer ski wear... just the world's first slalom slopes, still in their original condition and a valley where people have always loved to ski.
vest-telemark.museum.no

SKI DUBAI

Ski Dubai is the first indoor ski resort in the Middle East and offers an amazing snow setting to enjoy skiing, snowboarding and tobogganing, or just playing in the snow. Ski Dubai is a unique mountain-themed attraction that offers the opportunity to enjoy real snow in Dubai all year round. Ski Dubai has five runs that vary in difficulty, height and gradient, the longest run being 400 metres with a fall of over 60 metres. The ski resort is also the home of 20 snow penguins and the world's first indoor sub-zero zip line.
skidxb.com

GOPRO/MADISON

Supply robust personal action cameras that capture still and moving images of exceptional quality, which can be mounted almost anywhere on clothing or equipment.
madison.co.uk/gopro

LOWEPRO

Lowepro supply camera bags, without which it would be next to impossible to take all my camera gear up on the mountain.
lowepro.com

NOOKIE

Are makers of waterproof and thermal clothing.
nookie.co.uk

DEWERSTONE

Suppliers of outdoor lifestyle clothing to the discerning skier and climber.
dewerstone.com

ATOMIC SKIS

On-piste. in powder. at the X games. in the World Cup. wherever people ski, the best equipment comes from atomic – making skiing more exciting, more straightforward, more successful and more fun.

Every skier is different. Which is why Atomic provides every skier with skis, boots, bindings, helmets, protectors, poles – and now skiwear – built to exactly match his or her needs. Our aim is to help each skier have his or her ultimate skiing experience, whether they're all-mountain skiers, freeskiers or cross-country skiers, whether they want to win a World Cup race, have their sights set on new challenges in park and pipe, or live for action and fun in the powder.
atomic.com

PHOTOGRAPHERS:

Photographers/Photo © and credits:
T=top, B=bottom, L=left, R=right

All photos by and © Bill Mattos except:

p11 *TR*	Atomic / Mirja Geh
p12 *TL*	"Villa romana skier" by Kenton Greening. Licensed under Public domain via Wikimedia Commons
p13 2 × *TL*	Norwegian Ski Museum, Morgedal
p14	Atomic / Mirja Geh
p19, p22 *all*, p23 *TR*, p26 *TL*	Atomic
p22 *all*	Atomic
p28	Smuki / Dollar Photo Club
p34	Atomic
p35 *TR*, p36 *TR*, p37 *TL*	Atomic
p39 *TR*	Smuki / Dollar Photo Club
p39 *BL*, p42 *all*, p43 *BR*	Atomic
p45 *T*	James Weir
p47 *TL*	Wade Hindell
p52 *all*	Wade Hindell
p54/55 *all*, p56 *BR*	Syda Productions / Dollar Photo Club
p64 *TR*	Atomic / Mirja Geh, BL: Atomic
p70 *B*, p74 *TL*, p91 *TL*	James Weir
p95	FIS (International Ski Federation)
p126 *B*	Atomic
p130	A Rochau / Dollar Photo Club
p133	Greg / Dollar Photo Club
p134 *TL*	Atomic / Pondella, BR: Atomic Mirja Geh
p135	Oliver Weber / Dollar Photo Club
p137 *TR*	A Rochau / Dollar Photo Club, B: Atomic / Mirja Geh
p141 *TL*	Candybox Images / Dollar Photo Club
p146 *TL*	Atomic / Pondella
p148	Ron Fischer / Mariann Sæther
p152	Atomic
p153	Atomic / Mirja Geh
p155	R Caucino / Dollar Photo Club
p157 *B*	Stefano / Dollar Photo Club
p160 *all*	Ski Dubai
p161 *all*	Brad Waters
p162 *TL*	Joshua Gosling, TR: Tyler Olson / Dollar Photo Club, B: ITACE Expedition
p163	ITACE Expedition except R: Jenny Thomson / Dollar Photo Club
p164	Ron Fischer
p167	Atomic
p170 *TL*	Atomic / Hirscher, BR: Jon Wick / Wikimedia Commons
p176	Vistor Zastolski / Dollar Photo Club
p177	SZ / Dollar Photo Club
p179	Niklas Ramberg / Dollar Photo Club
p180 *all*	Atomic / Magnus Oesth, except BR: Atomic / Anders Aukland
p181	Atomic / Mirja Geh
p182	Ron Fischer / Mariann Sæther

TOP TEN TIPS

Most of these are things that I never figured out when I used to go on occasional ski holidays, but have become abundantly clear to me since living in the mountains:

1 Start early. Even if you aren't a morning person. Once the sun is on the slopes, things get worse, not better.

2 Know when to quit. Being exhausted is only a nice feeling after you get off the hill.

3 If you are the sort of person who likes to look good at things, ski well on moderate slopes instead of fumbling down ones that are too steep. You can spot whether someone is carving beautifully or flailing from *literally* a mile away. Maybe further.

4 Try other things. Go cross-country skiing, snowshoeing, skidooing, husky sledding, igloo building. The week in which you spend a day on each of many snow sports is a lot more fulfilling than the one in which you are whimpering with hire-boot fuelled agony by day four.

5 Get your head around different coloured goggle lenses. Being able to see in all conditions is so cool!

6 Take water on the hill with you. Skiing is thirsty work and paying crazy money for bottled water on the mountain makes me sad. I like a Camelbak™ hydration thingy with a tube. Insulate the tube with pipe lagging, or it will freeze!

7 Attach leashes/lanyards to things. Camera, phone, wallet, keys, gloves...

8 Winter tyres are awesome. Chains are evil, horrible things.

9 Get some really good, snow compatible footwear. Wet feet ruin a night out.

10 Don't blindly follow someone's tracks unless you can see where they end...